Comprehensive Ea

Professional Series

Level 6

Carol Schlosar

Library and Archives Canada Cataloguing in Publication

Schlosar, Carol, 1955-

—Comprehensive ear training [music] / Carol Schlosar.

To be complete in 10 volumes; each v. is accompanied by 2 compact discs.
Also available without compact discs, or with sound recordings in other formats.
Levels 1-2 — Level 3 — Level 4 — Level 5 — Level 6 — Level 7 — Level 8 — Level 9 — Level 10 — Level 11/ARCT.

ISBN 978-1-55440-124-6 (levels 1-2)
ISBN 978-1-55440-125-3 (level 3)
ISBN 978-1-55440-126-0 (level 4)
ISBN 978-1-55440-127-7 (level 5)
ISBN 978-1-55440-128-4 (level 6)
ISBN 978-1-55440-129-1 (level 7)
ISBN 978-1-55440-130-7 (level 8)
ISBN 978-1-55440-131-4 (level 9)
ISBN 978-1-55440-132-1 (level 10)
ISBN 978-1-55440-133-8 (level 11/ARCT)

1. Ear training—Problems, exercises, etc. 2. Musical meter and rhythm—Studies and exercises. I. Title.
MT35.S558 2007 781.4'24 C2007-904791-2

16 15 14 13 12 11 10 09 08 07 1 2 3 4 5 6 7 8 9 10

FREDERICK HARRIS MUSIC

Developing critical listening skills is one of the most important aspects of musical training, whether it be in preparation for examinations and auditions, or for expanding overall musical capabilities. It is often the most neglected as well. For the teacher there is rarely enough time to cover everything in a lesson and for the student, a regular program of ear training is often difficult to establish.

COMPREHENSIVE EAR TRAINING has the perfect solution. Whether you have purchased the Book, Book/CDs, or Book/Disk set, with these powerful learning tools ear training becomes manageable and enjoyable.

The ***COMPREHENSIVE EAR TRAINING*** series features:

- an easy to follow format with clear step- by- step instructions
- plenty of exercises to ensure success
- all requirements for each grade in every Session
- choice of formats--

  Professional Series: Book & 2 CD set, Book & SMF Disk set or Book only

  Student Series: Single CD with answer booklet

COMPREHENSIVE EAR TRAINING is ideal for students in private or group lessons and for those in self study programs. The learning environment is stress free as each student proceeds at their own pace.

The aim of this program is to develop musical potential with a firm foundation in ear training at each grade level. Following this series will give students the skill and confidence to succeed.

Contents

*Note: The current syllabus for practical examinations should be consulted to ensure that all ear training requirements are met.

Ear Training Practice Tips

One of the most important keys to learning is repetition, so practice is essential. Ear training is like a muscle- it needs exercise and the more you use, it the stronger you are! For the best results, ear training should be done on a regular basis throughout the year.

Rhythm Clapback Exercises

1. You need a firm grasp of note values and their relationships. Start by sight reading blank rhythms and then move to simple rhythmic dictation. The exercises in this book and in earlier grades are a very useful tools for rhythmic dictation.
2. Start by beating time with the music to find the rhythmic pulse. Sing the tune then clap or tap the rhythm.
3. Listen carefully for emphasis on the first beat of each measure. This will help you with the rhythmic pulse.
4. Often melodic-rhythmic passages (such as those given at exams) have too many elements to analyze at one time and it is easy to be overwhelmed. Break the concepts into smaller parts. Start by having someone clap just the rhythm pattern. Then move to clapping back a rhythm played on single note and, once you are confident, move onto clapback exercises with a melody.
5. New rhythmic elements are introduced at different grade levels. Special attention should be paid to ensure that you have a theoretical understanding of these rhythmic concepts before starting the rhythm clap backs. Make sure you understand how these notes relate to the other note values and how they relate in the framework of the beat.

Interval Identification

1. Practice intervals by playing or singing the first note, and then singing the second note. This promotes "active listening"and if you can sing the interval, you can identify the interval.
2. Start by singing all the required intervals above or below the same note. Once this is comfortable, then change the starting note with each interval.
3. Visualize the written distance and the spatial distance when singing the intervals to establish the relationships between sight and sound. Also, when working on a piece of music, identify the intervals by size and quality and relate that to the sound of the interval.
4. Knowledge of intervals should based on foundation of scales and chords but familiar tunes may help to reinforce interval memory (Minor 3rd above: O Canada, , Minor 3rd below: This Old Man).

New intervals for Grade 6 are

Major 2nd Above (helpful song: "Silent Night", "Brother John")
Perfect 4th Below (helpful songs: "Old McDonald", "Baseball Chant")
Minor 6th Below (helpful song "Love Story Theme")

Chord Identification

1. To help distinguish between major and minor triads, start by focusing on the difference between major 3rd and minor 3rd intervals and then move to triads.
2. Listen for the sound quality and tension of the chord - major has a happier sound while minor is more mysterious or sad.
3. Listen and compare all chords starting on the same note. Example; C major and C minor triads. Practice singing them as broken chords.
4. Sing the individual notes of the chords after the solid chord is played, aloud at first, and then singing them silently.

New for Grade 6 is the identification of major and minor triads in root position.

Melody Playback

1. Listen carefully to the tonic chord. This establishes tonality and helps you to find the starting note (one of the notes of the chord). Visualize the key signature of the key and placement of those accidentals on the keyboard.
2. Most important is to retain a "visual memory" of the note movement. Ask these questions as the passage is being played. Which direction do the notes move? Do the notes move by step or larger intervals? Are the notes repeated? Mentally draw a pitch direction line.
3. What are the rhythm patterns? Practice rhythmic diction to reinforce this skill.
4. Singing the melody helps to support the "memory" required to play back the phrase successfully.

How to Use *Comprehensive Ear Training*

The ***Comprehensive Ear Training*** Series includes

INTRODUCTORY EXERCISES to introduce the new material for each grade level
SESSIONS (48 practice sets) that include :
- 2 Rhythm Clapback exercises
- 8 Interval Identification exercises
- 6 Chord Identification exercises
- 2 Melody Playback exercises

ADDITIONAL EXERCISES that target problem areas
WORKSHEETS with space to answer questions and score your work

This series is best used with the CDs, Standard MIDI file disk, or with a teacher or parent to play the exercises. If you are working without this support, follow the instructions "Using Book Only Exercises" on the next page.

1. Open the book to the Worksheets on pages 38-43 and select a session (Example from Session 1). By checking your answers and recording your marks, you will have a more accurate picture of your progress and areas that can be improved.

Session 1
Page 10
Track 2

Score /40

Rhythm Clapback	1	2
	3/4	2/4

Interval Identification	1	2	3	4	5	6	7	8

Chord Identification	1	2	3	4	5	6

Melody Playback	1	2
	F major	C major

2. Find the Exercise Session in the Book, on the CD, or Disk and start the Session using the directions below.

Rhythm Clapback Exercises: (Example from Session 1)

Look at the worksheet and identify the time signature. Listen carefully as the teacher, CD, or disk plays the rhythm twice. Stop the playback. Imitate the rhythm pattern by clapping, tapping or singing. Check your answers with the book. Award a score of 5 points for each correct answer (maximum of 10 points). These exercises can also be used for Rhythmic Dictation.

Interval Identification Exercises: (Example from Session 1)

minor 3A   minor 6B   perfect 4A   major 2A   perfect 8B   perfect 5A   minor 3A   major 6A

Listen carefully as the teacher, CD, or disk plays each interval once. Stop the playback. Identify the interval by quality (major), size (3) and whether the second note is above (A) or below (B) the first note (intervals for this grade are listed below). Write your answers in the space provided on the worksheet. Check your answers with the book and award 1 point for each correct answer (total of 8 points).

Above a given note:		Below a given note:	
Major Second	Perfect Fifth	Minor Third	Perfect Fifth
Minor Third	Minor Sixth	Major Third	Minor Sixth
Major Third	Major Sixth	Perfect Fourth	Perfect Octave
Perfect Fourth	Perfect Octave		

Chord Identification Exercises: (Example from Session 1)

major minor minor major minor major

Listen carefully as the teacher, CD or disk plays each triad (3 note chord) once in root position. Stop the play back. Identify the chord as major or minor. Write your answers in the space provided on the worksheet. Check your answers with the book and award 2 points for each correct answer (maximum of 12 points).

Melody Playback Exercises: (Example from Session 1)

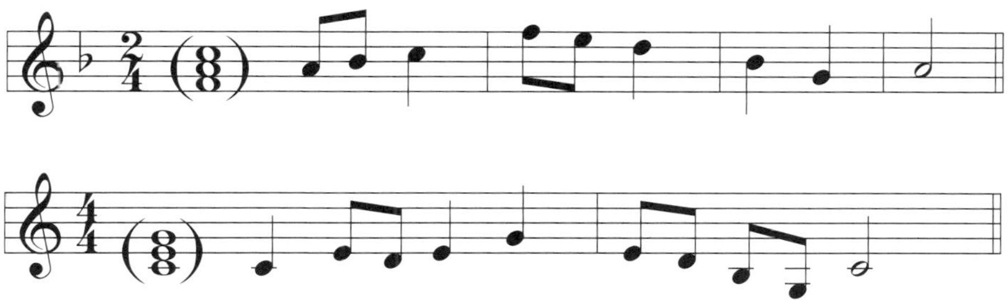

Look at the worksheet and identify the key signature (C, F, G or D major). Listen carefully as the teacher, CD, or disk plays the tonic triad once, then plays the melody twice. Stop the playback. Play the melody from memory. The melody is approximately nine notes long and is based on the complete major scale from tonic (1st note) to tonic or dominant (5th note) to dominant. The melody may start on the tonic (1st note), mediant (3rd note), or the dominant (5th note). Check your answers with the book. Award 5 points for each correct answer (maximum of 10 points). These exercises can also be used for Melodic Dictation.

Score: Add up the total points and award a final score out of 40 points for each Session. Keep your Worksheets on file to measure your improvement.

Using "Book Only" Exercises (no CD or Disk)

Open the book to the chosen exercise (worksheets will not be used). Begin the exercise using the following instructions.

Rhythm Clapback Exercises
Using the book, note the time signature. Clap, tap or sing the rhythm while reading the music then repeat from memory.

Interval Identification Exercises
Using the book, play both notes of the interval, listening carefully. Sing both notes from memory and identify the interval by quality (major) , size (3rd) and whether the second note is above (A) or below (B) the first note.

Chord Identification Exercises
Using the book, play the chord, listening carefully. Sing the notes (in broken form) then check your accuracy by playing these notes again. Identify each chord as major or minor.

Melody Playback Exercises
Using the book, note the key signature. Play the tonic chord once, then play the phrase twice. Sing or hum the melody then play it back from memory.

Introductory Exercises

Rhythm Clapback - Rhythms for Grade Six are based on the note values 𝅘𝅥𝅯 𝅘𝅥𝅮 𝅘𝅥𝅮. 𝅘𝅥 𝅗𝅥 𝅗𝅥. in $\frac{2}{4}$, $\frac{3}{4}$, and $\frac{6}{8}$

Interval Identification - New intervals used in Grade Six are major 2A, perfect 4B and minor 6B. Here they are presented with closely related intervals.

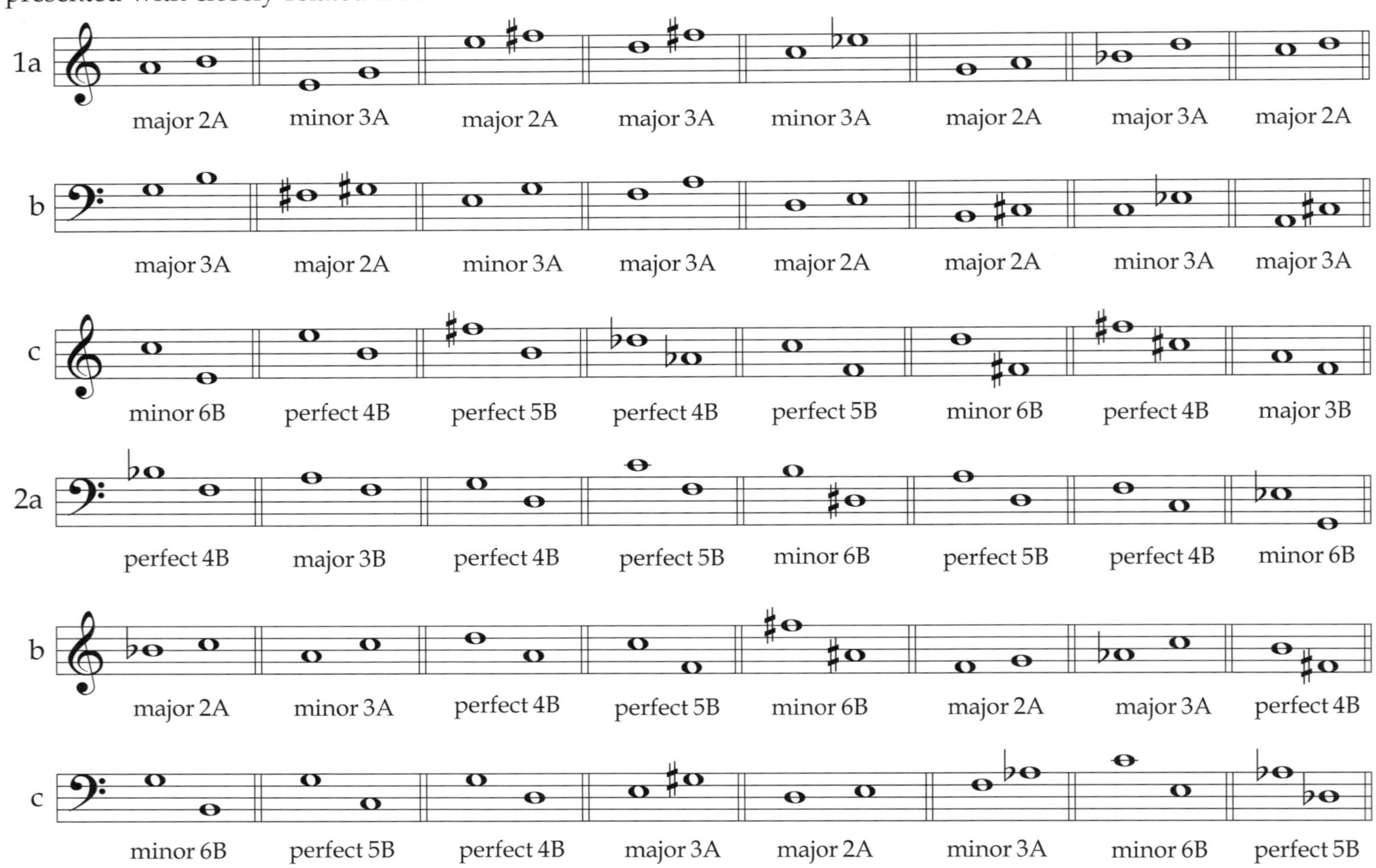

Introductory Exercises

Chords Identification - New for Grade Six is the identification of major or minor triads (3 note chords) in solid form (the chords are shown here in broken and then in solid form).

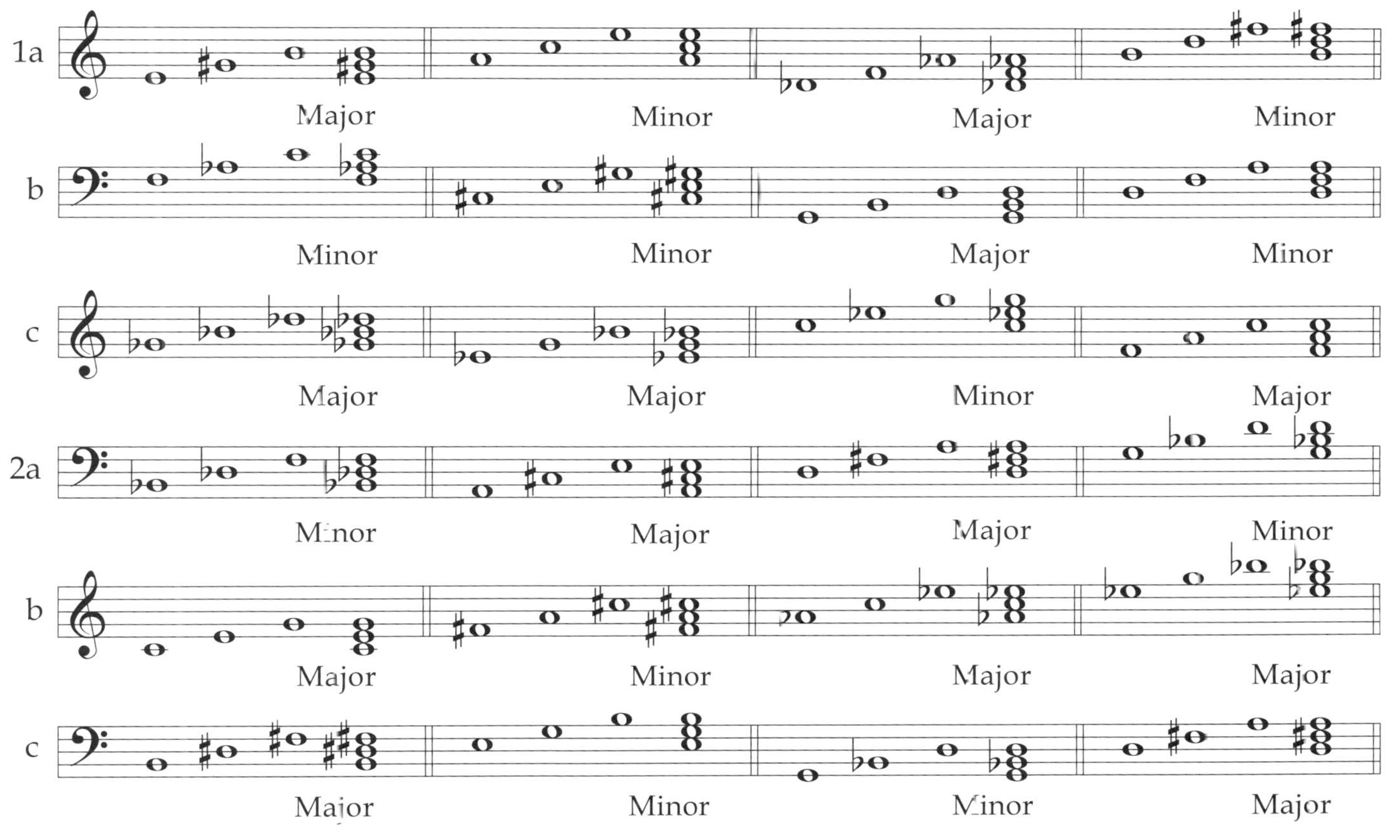

Melody Playbacks - New approach for Grade Six is the use of the complete major scale from tonic to tonic (1st note of scale) or dominant to dominant (5th note of the scale).

Session 1

A Rhythm Clapback

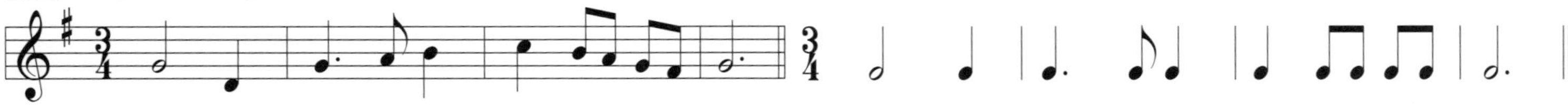

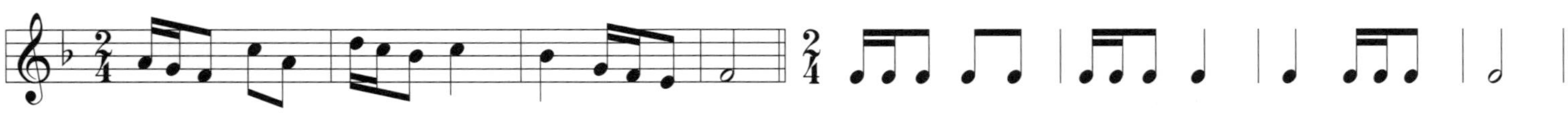

B Interval Identification

minor 3A | minor 6B | perfect 4A | major 2A | perfect 8B | perfect 5A | minor 3A | major 6A

C Chord Identification

major | minor | minor | major | minor | major

D Melody Playback

Session 2

A Rhythm Clapback

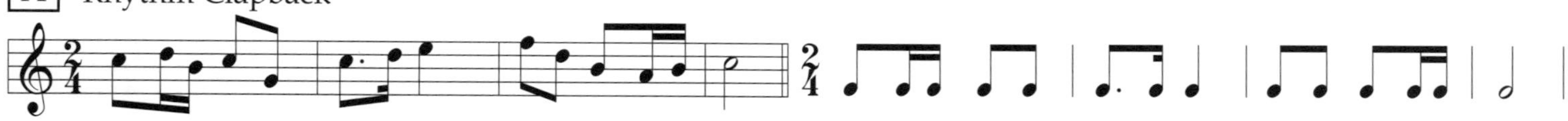

B Interval Identification

minor 3B | minor 6A | perfect 5A | perfect 4B | minor 3A | perfect 4B | major 6A | perfect 5B

C Chord Identification

minor | major | minor | minor | major | major

D Melody Playback

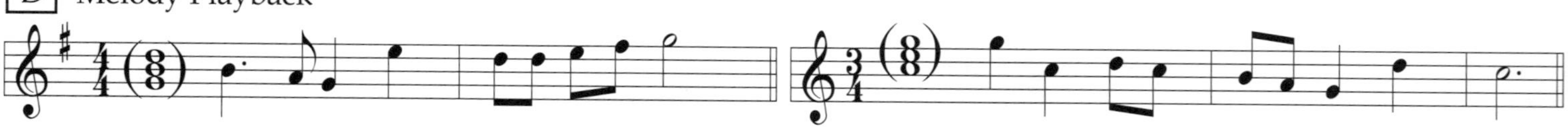

Session 3

A Rhythm Clapback

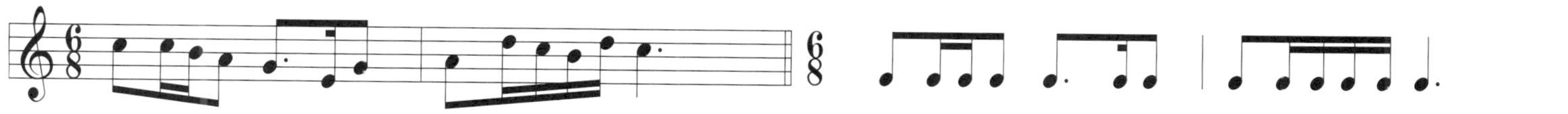

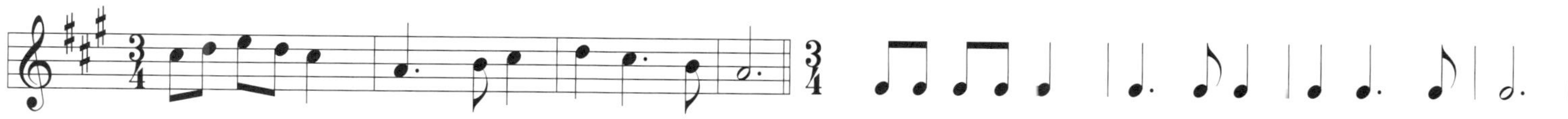

B Interval Identification

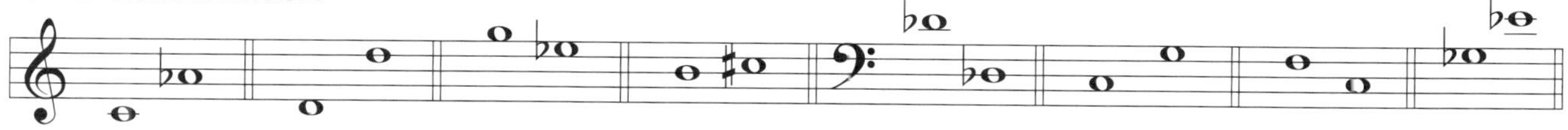

minor 6A | perfect 8A | major 3B | major 2A | perfect 8B | perfect 5A | perfect 4B | major 6A

C Chord Identification

major | major | minor | minor | minor | major

D Melody Playback

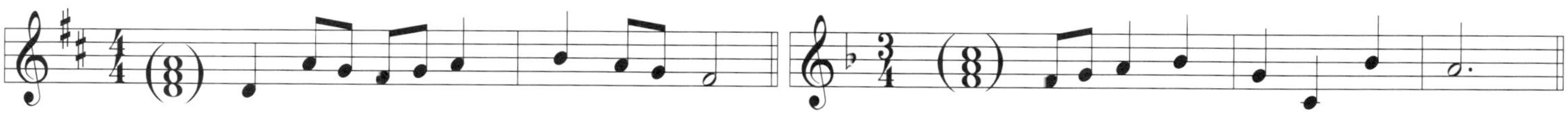

Session 4

A Rhythm Clapback

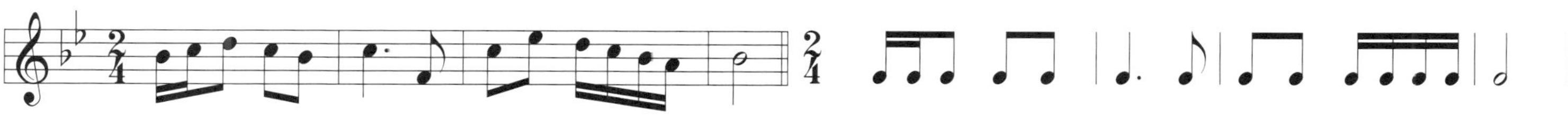

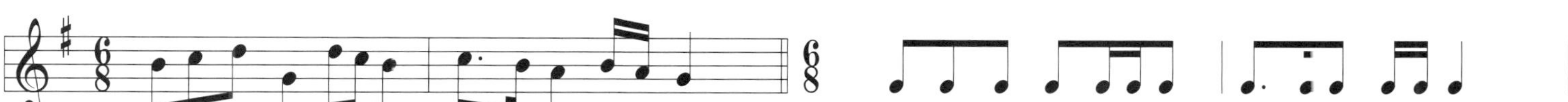

B Interval Identification

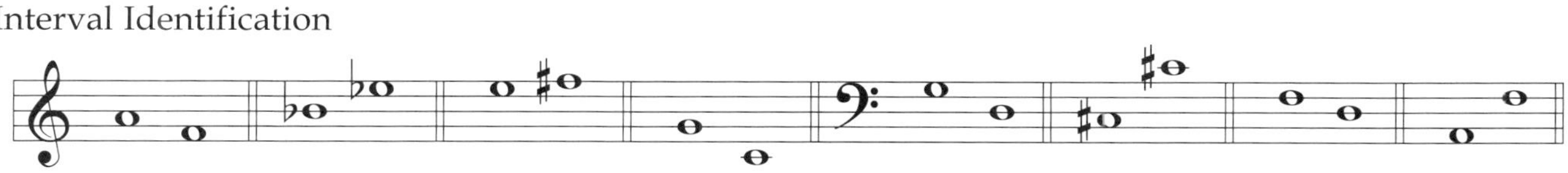

major 3B | perfect 4A | major 2A | perfect 5B | perfect 4B | perfect 8A | minor 3B | minor 6A

C Chord Identification

minor | major | minor | major | major | minor

D Melody Playback

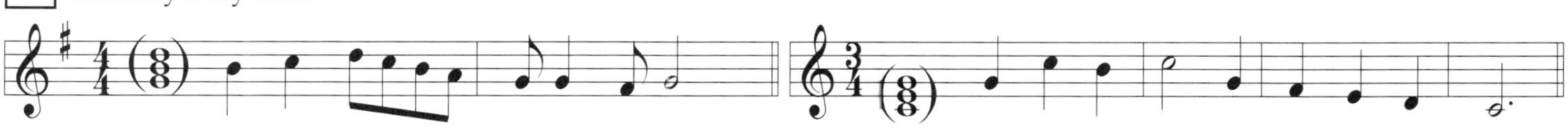

Session 5

A Rhythm Clapback

B Interval Identification

C Chord Identification

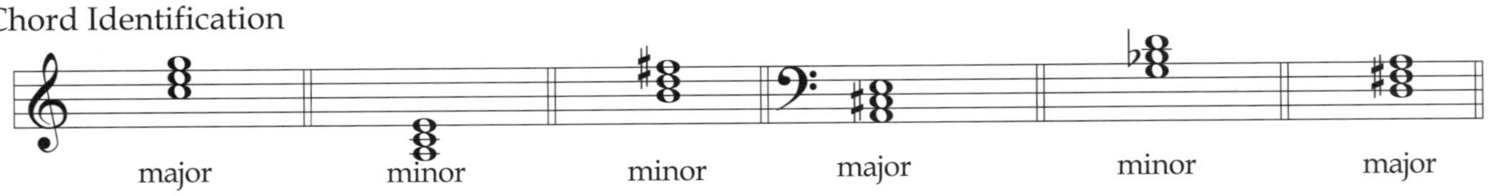

D Melody Playback

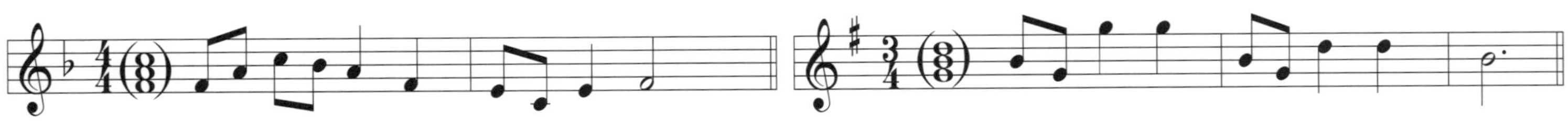

Session 6

A Rhythm Clapback

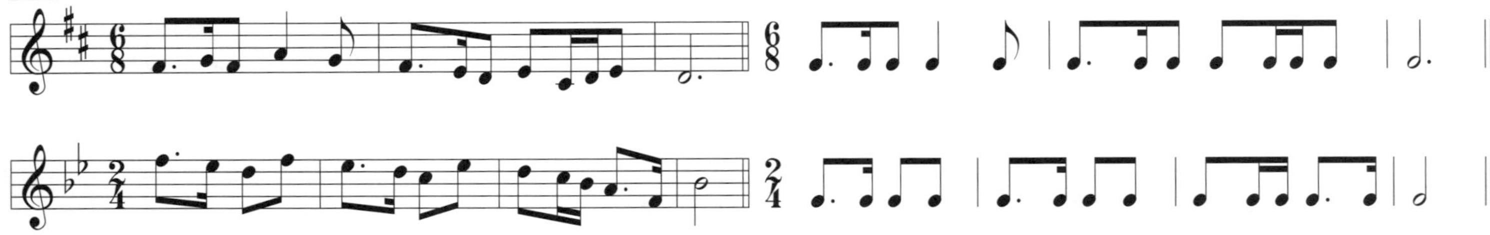

B Interval Identification

C Chord Identification

D Melody Playback

Session 7

A Rhythm Clapback

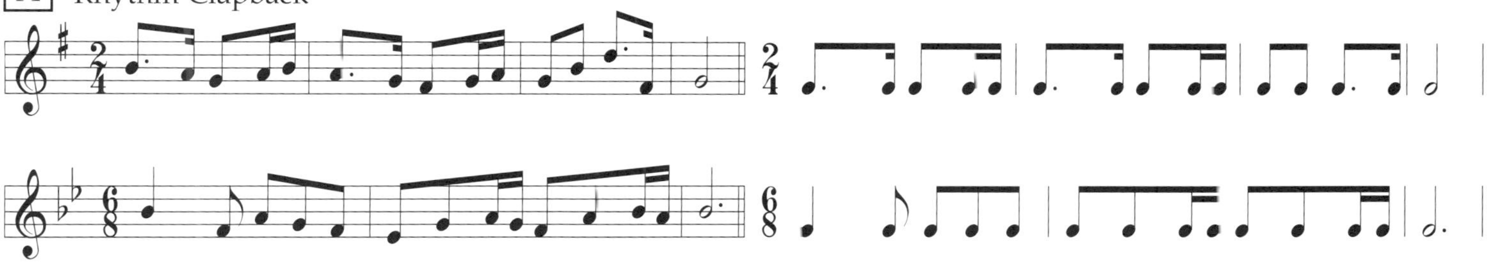

B Interval Identification

minor 6B | minor 3A | perfect 5A | major 2A | minor 3B | perfect 5B | perfect 4A | major 3B

C Chord Identification

major | major | major | major | major | major

D Melody Playback

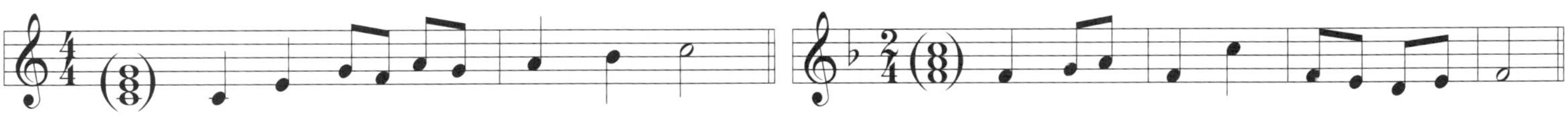

Session 8

A Rhythm Clapback

B Interval Identification

major 3A | perfect 8A | perfect 4B | minor 6A | perfect 4A | minor 6B | perfect 8B | major 2A

C Chord Identification

minor | minor | major | minor | major | minor

D Melody Playback

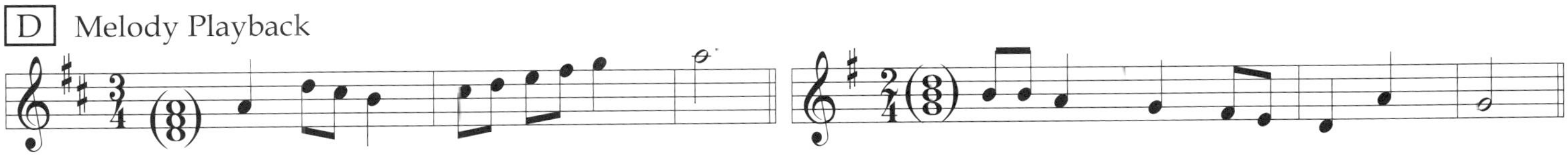

Session 9

A Rhythm Clapback

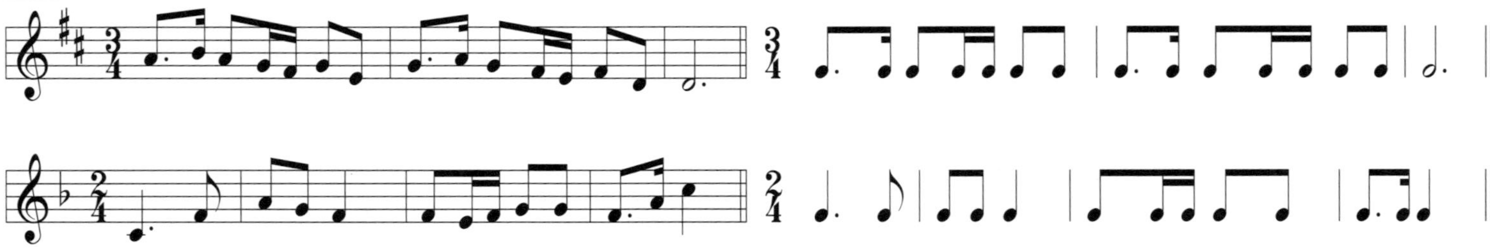

B Interval Identification

perfect 5A | minor 3B | major 2A | perfect 4B | major 6A | minor 6B | major 3B | perfect 4A

C Chord Identification

major | minor | major | minor | major | minor

D Melody Playback

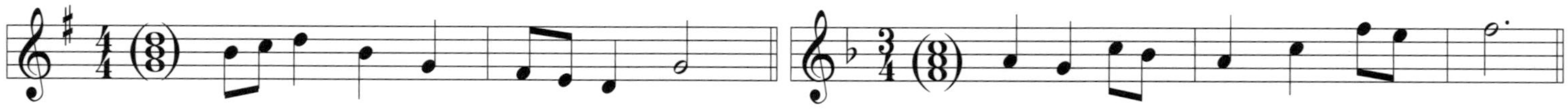

Session 10

A Rhythm Clapback

B Interval Identification

perfect 8B | major 3A | perfect 8A | perfect 5B | minor 3A | perfect 4B | major 2A | major 3B

C Chord Identification

major | major | minor | minor | major | minor

D Melody Playback

Session 11

A Rhythm Clapback

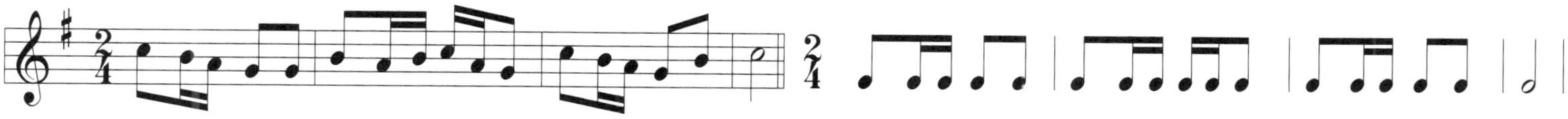

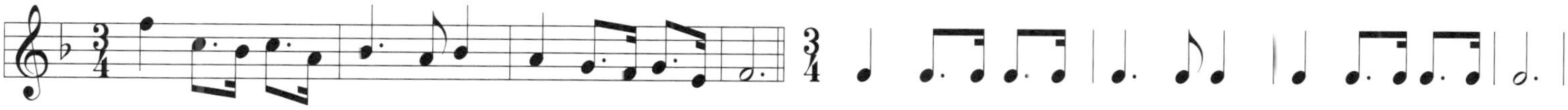

B Interval Identification

perfect 5B | minor 3B | major 6A | minor 6A | major 3B | perfect 5A | minor 6B | perfect 4B

C Chord Identification

minor | major | minor | major | major | minor

D Melody Playback

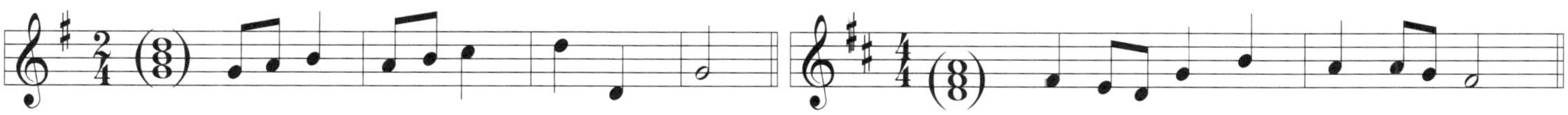

Session 12

A Rhythm Clapback

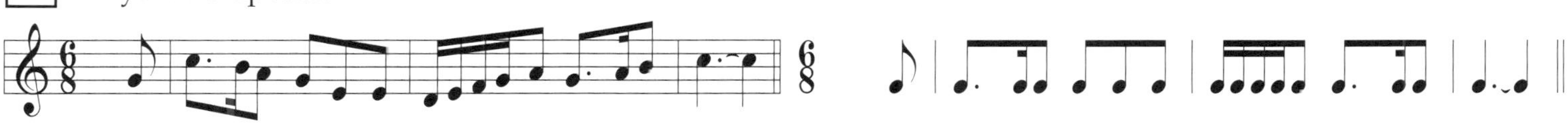

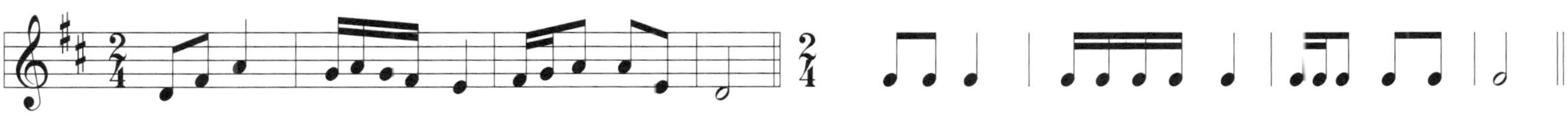

B Interval Identification

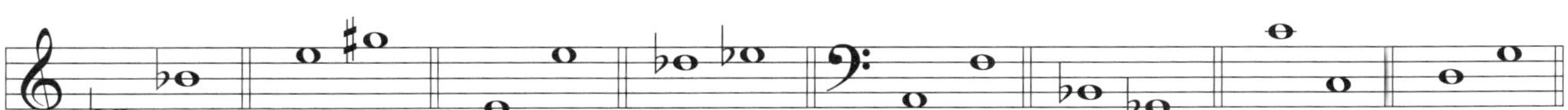

major 6A | major 3A | perfect 8A | major 2A | minor 6A | major 3B | perfect 8B | perfect 4A

C Chord Identification

major | major | minor | minor | major | minor

D Melody Playback

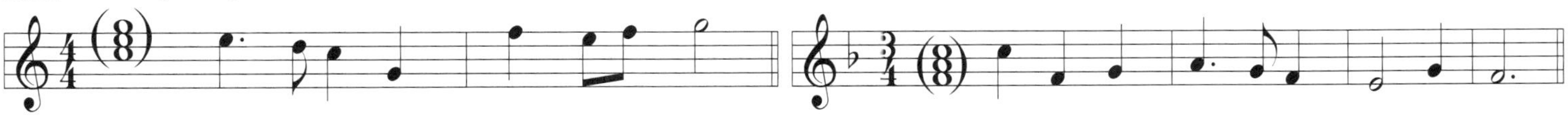

Session 13

A Rhythm Clapback

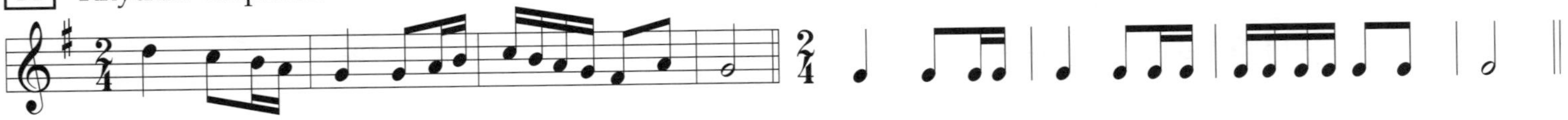

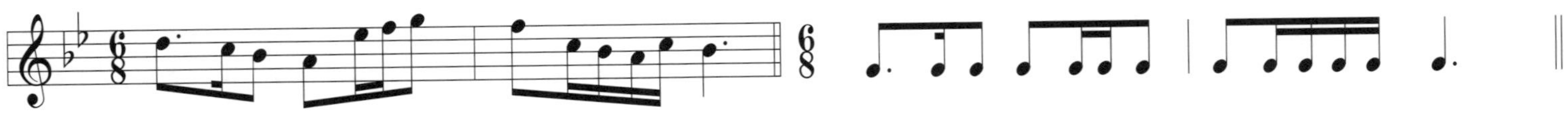

B Interval Identification

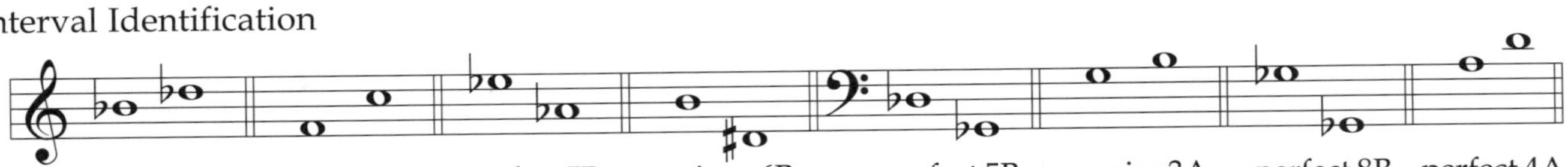

minor 3A | perfect 5A | perfect 5B | minor 6B | perfect 5B | major 3A | perfect 8B | perfect 4A

C Chord Identification

major | minor | major | major | minor | major

D Melody Playback

Session 14

A Rhythm Clapback

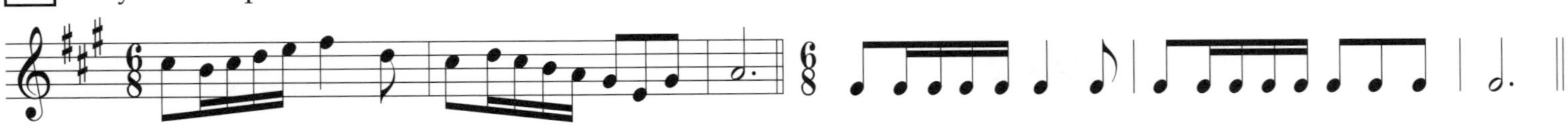

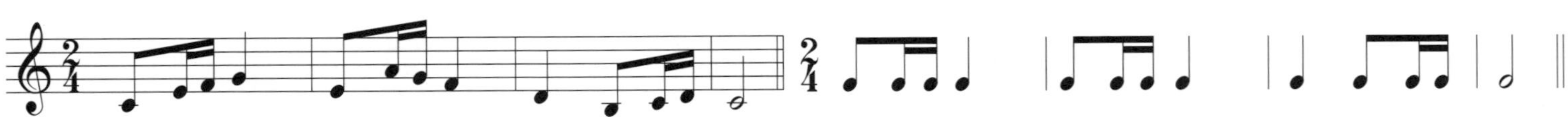

B Interval Identification

perfect 4A | perfect 8B | major 2A | perfect 8A | perfect 4B | minor 6A | perfect 5A | minor 3B

C Chord Identification

major | minor | minor | minor | major | major

D Melody Playback

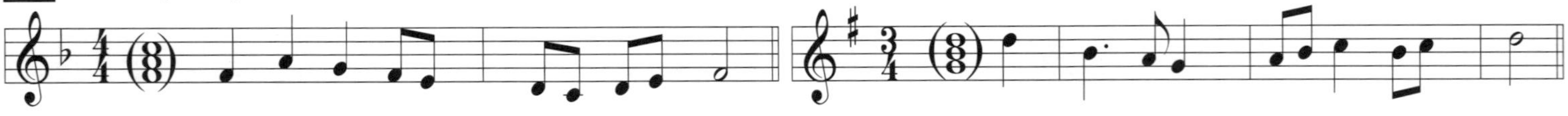

Session 15

A Rhythm Clapback

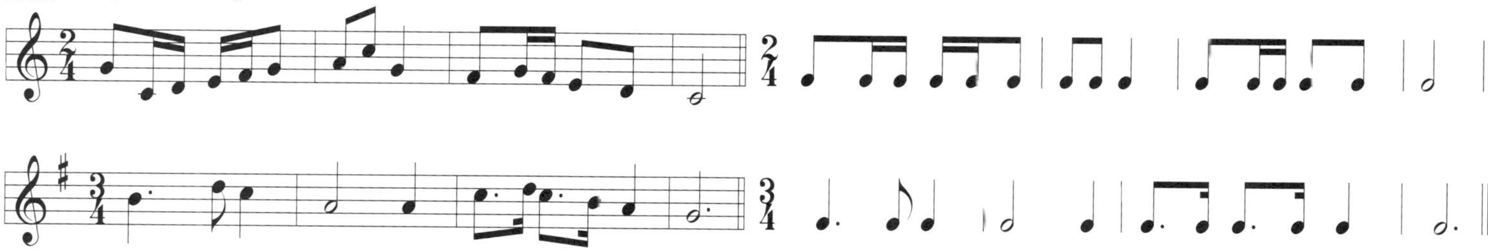

B Interval Identification

C Chord Identification

D Melody Playback

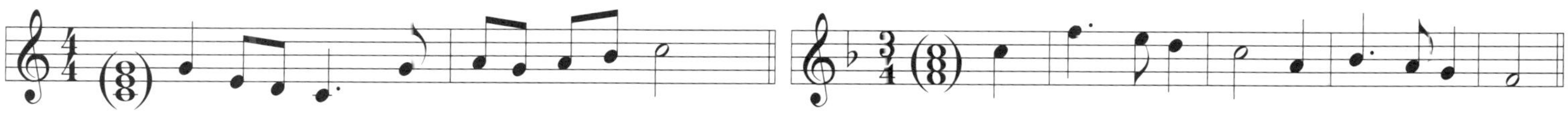

Session 16

A Rhythm Clapback

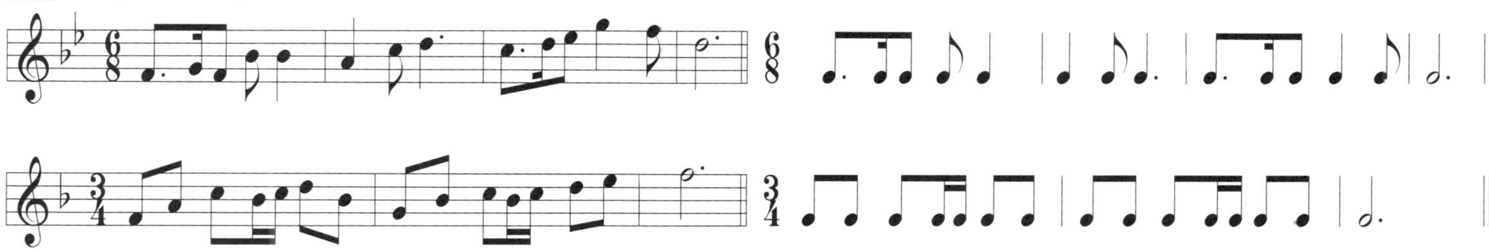

B Interval Identification

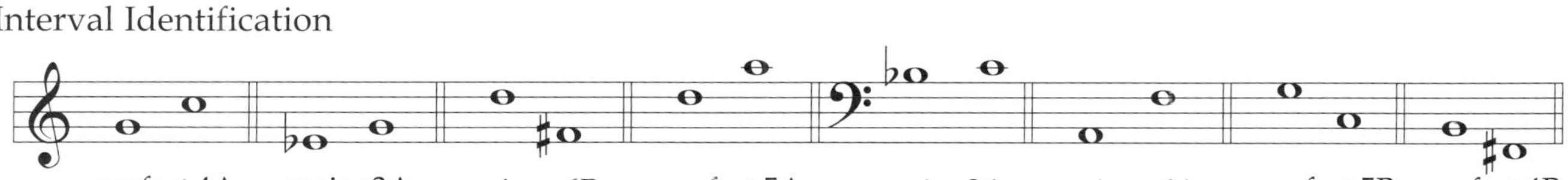

C Chord Identification

D Melody Playback

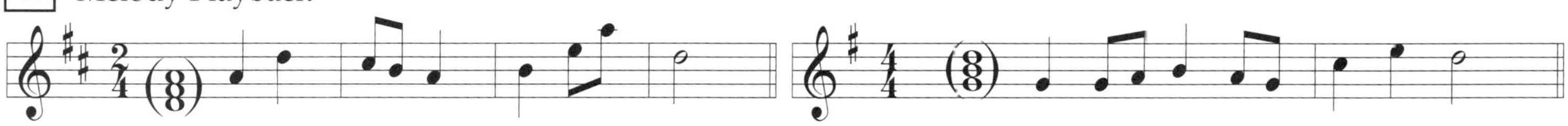

Session 17

A Rhythm Clapback

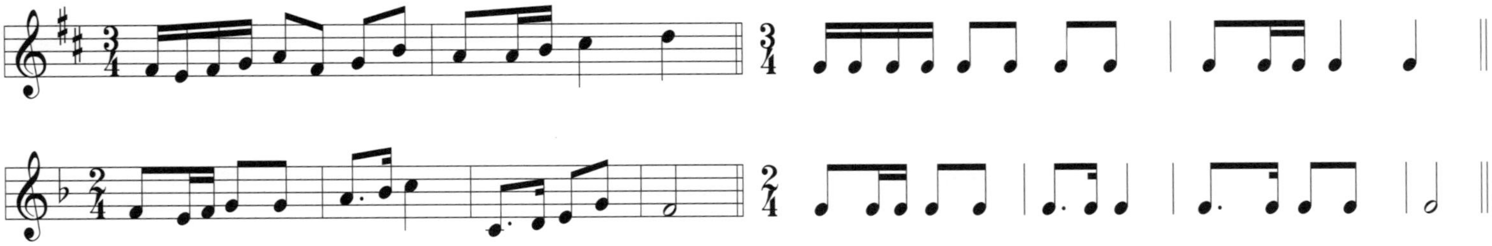

B Interval Identification

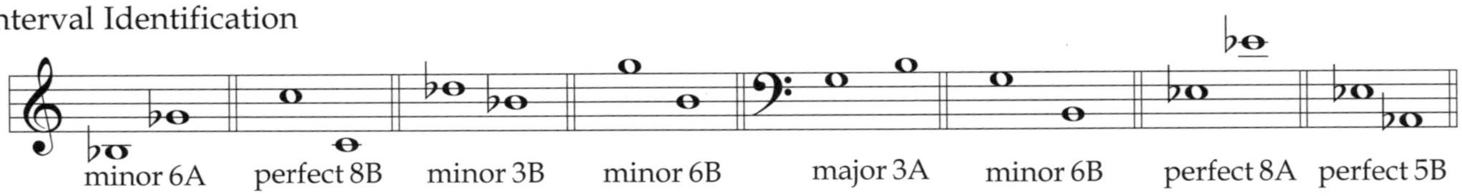

C Chord Identification

D Melody Playback

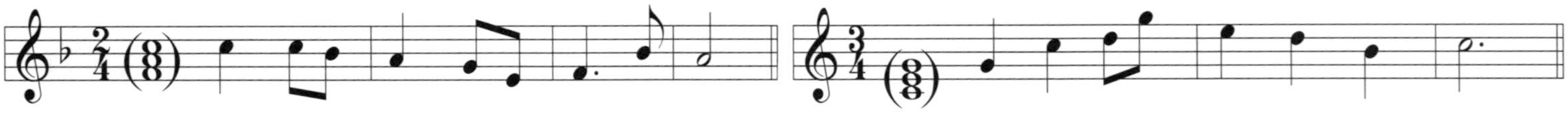

Session 18

A Rhythm Clapback

B Interval Identification

C Chord Identification

D Melody Playback

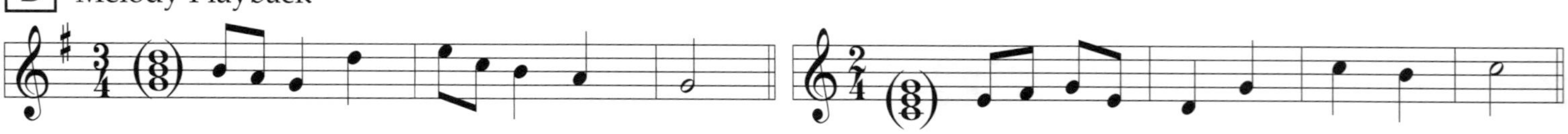

Session 19

A Rhythm Clapback

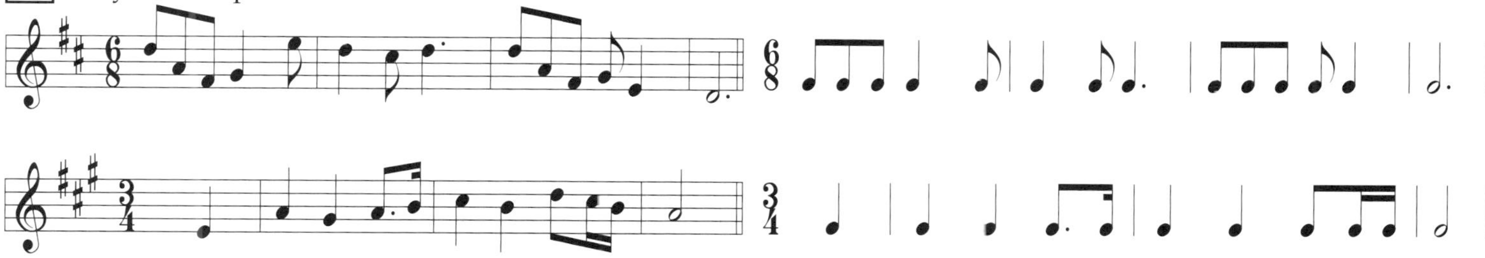

B Interval Identification

major 6A | perfect 5B | major 2A | minor 6B | perfect 4A | perfect 4B | minor 3A | major 3B

C Chord Identification

minor | major | major | major | minor | major

D Melody Playback

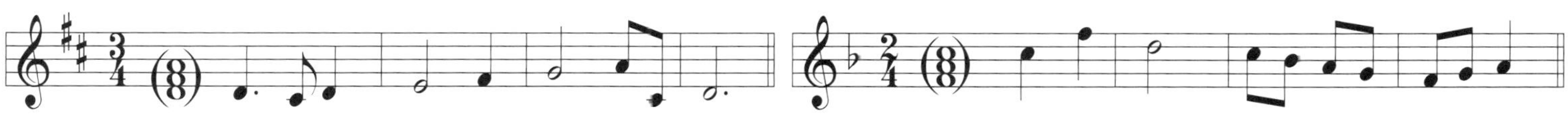

Session 20

A Rhythm Clapback

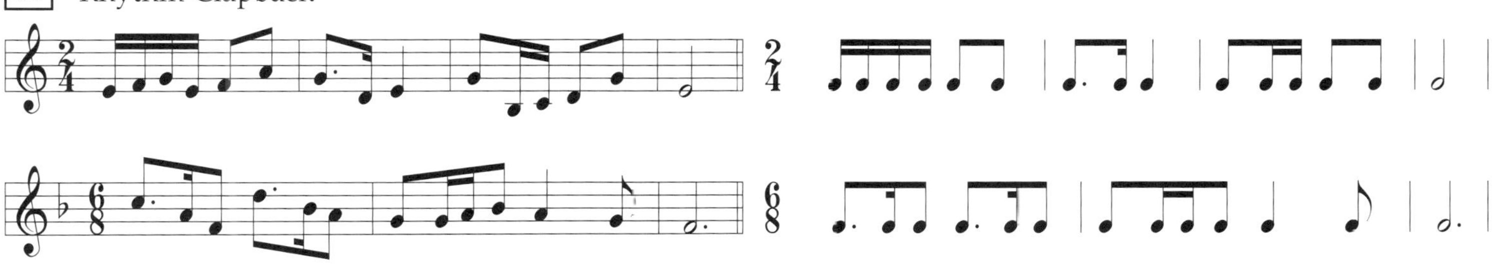

B Interval Identification

perfect 8B | minor 3B | perfect 5A | minor 6A | perfect 5B | perfect 8A | major 3B | major 6A

C Chord Identification

minor | minor | major | minor | major | major

D Melody Playback

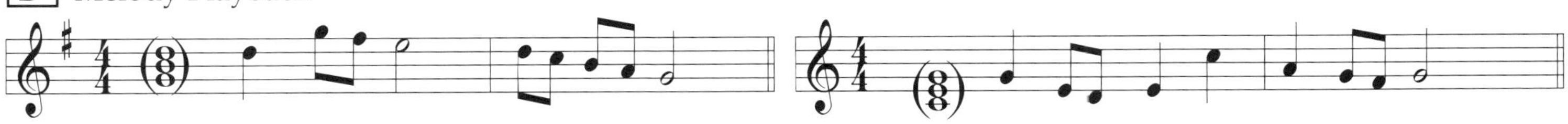

Session 21

A Rhythm Clapback

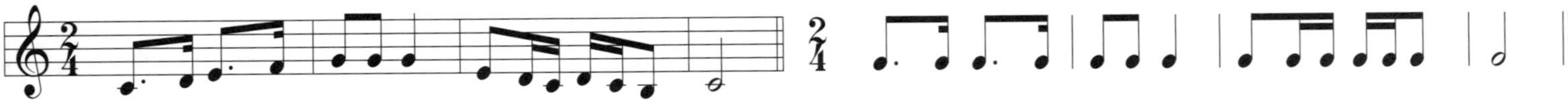

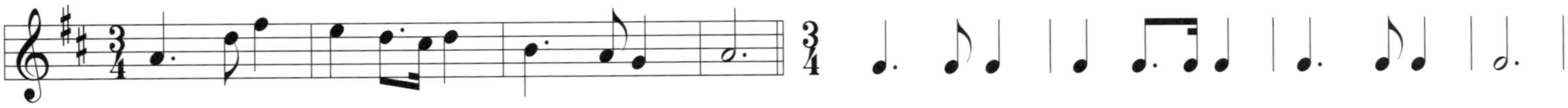

B Interval Identification

minor 3A | perfect 4B | major 2A | minor 6B | major 3B | perfect 4A | minor 6A | perfect 5B

C Chord Identification

major | minor | major | minor | minor | major

D Melody Playback

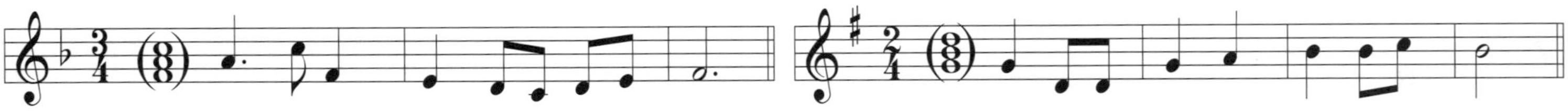

Session 22

A Rhythm Clapback

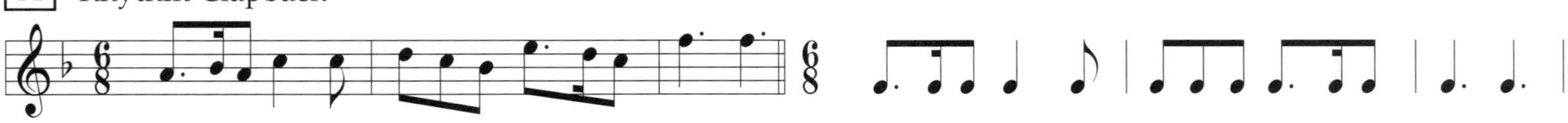

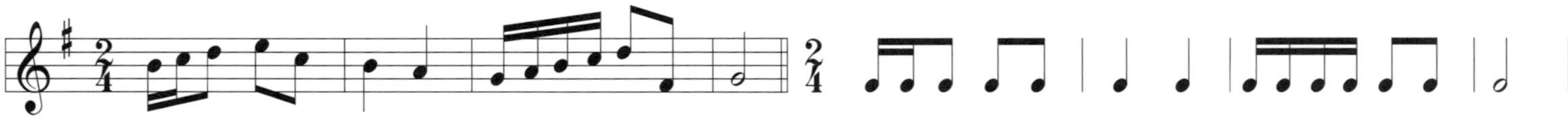

B Interval Identification

perfect 8A | major 3B | perfect 5A | perfect 4B | minor 6A | minor 3B | perfect 8B | major 3A

C Chord Identification

major | major | major | major | minor | minor

D Melody Playback

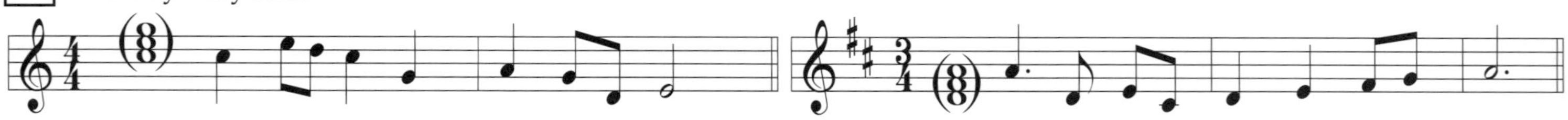

Session 23

A Rhythm Clapback

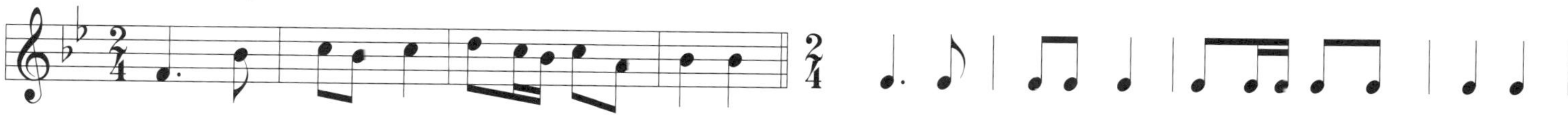

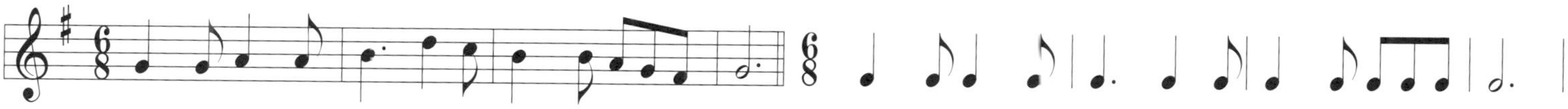

B Interval Identification

major 6A | minor 3B | perfect 5B | major 2A | minor 6A | minor 3A | perfect 4B | major 3B

C Chord Identification

minor | major | minor | minor | major | major

D Melody Playback

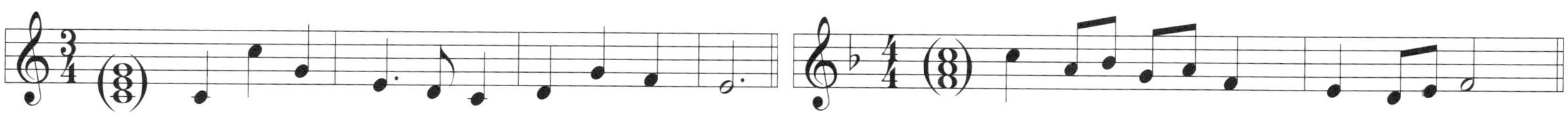

Session 24

A Rhythm Clapback

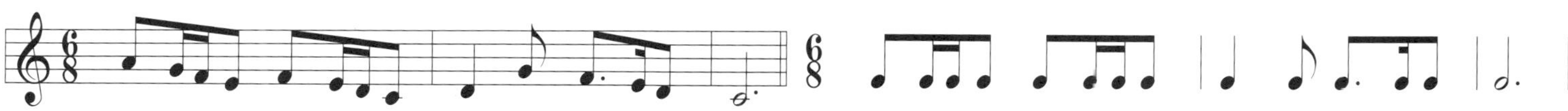

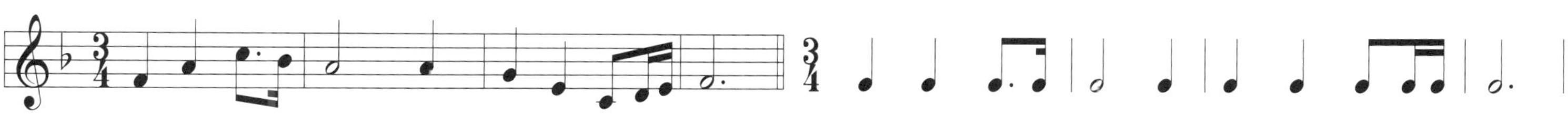

B Interval Identification

perfect 4A | minor 6A | perfect 8B | major 3B | perfect 5B | perfect 8A | major 6A | perfect 4B

C Chord Identification

major | minor | major | major | minor | major

D Melody Playback

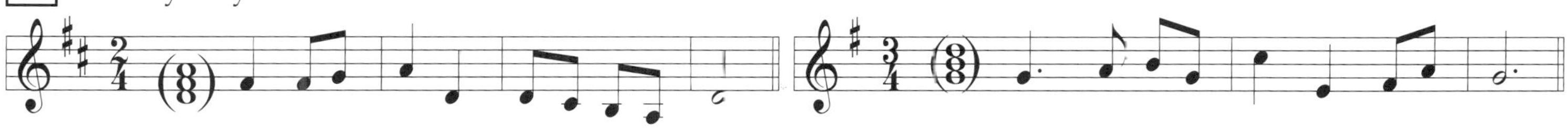

Session 25

A Rhythm Clapback

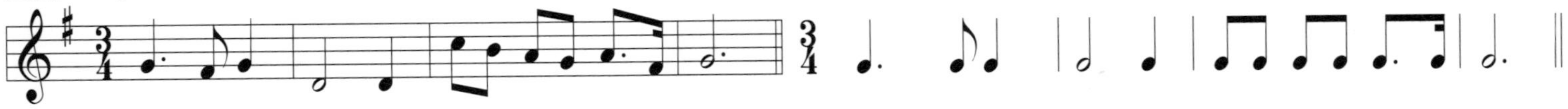

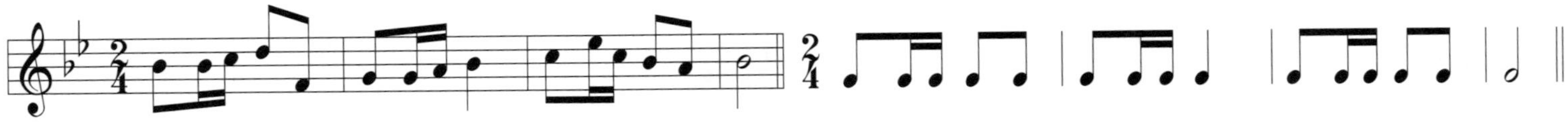

B Interval Identification

perfect 4B | perfect 5A | major 2A | minor 3B | perfect 5A | minor 6B | minor 6A | major 3B

C Chord Identification

major | minor | major | minor | major | minor

D Melody Playback

Session 26

A Rhythm Clapback

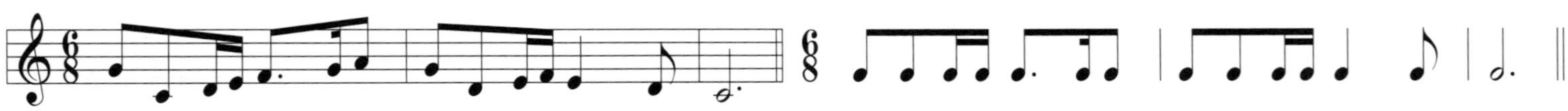

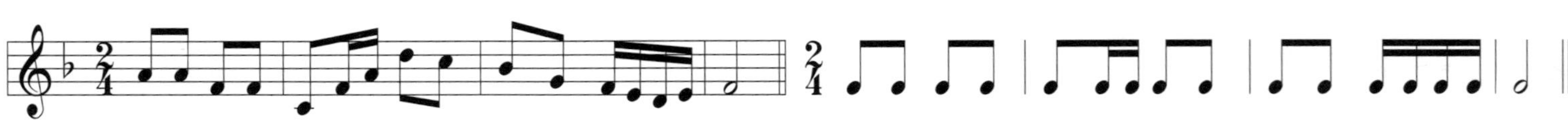

B Interval Identification

minor 6B | perfect 8B | major 3A | minor 3A | perfect 8A | perfect 5A | minor 3B | perfect 4B

C Chord Identification

major | major | minor | minor | major | minor

D Melody Playback

Session 27

A Rhythm Clapback

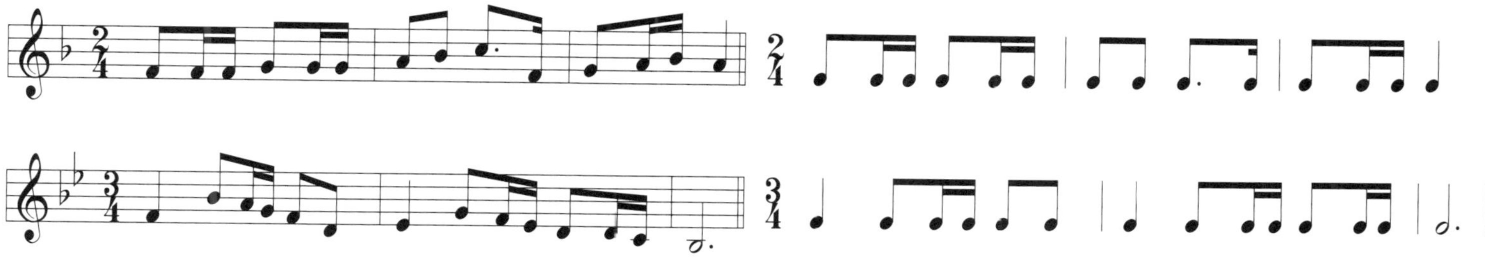

B Interval Identification

minor 6B | perfect 4A | major 3A | perfect 8B | major 6A | minor 3B | minor 6A | perfect 5A

C Chord Identification

major | major | major | major | minor | major

D Melody Playback

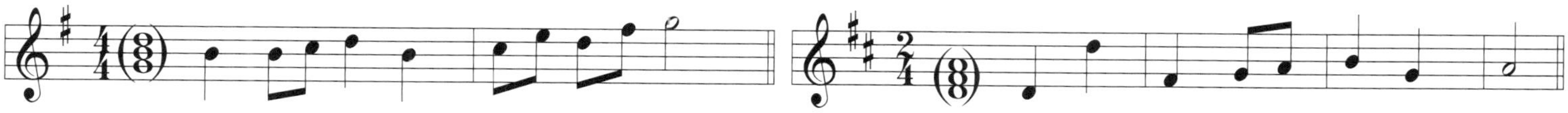

Session 28

A Rhythm Clapback

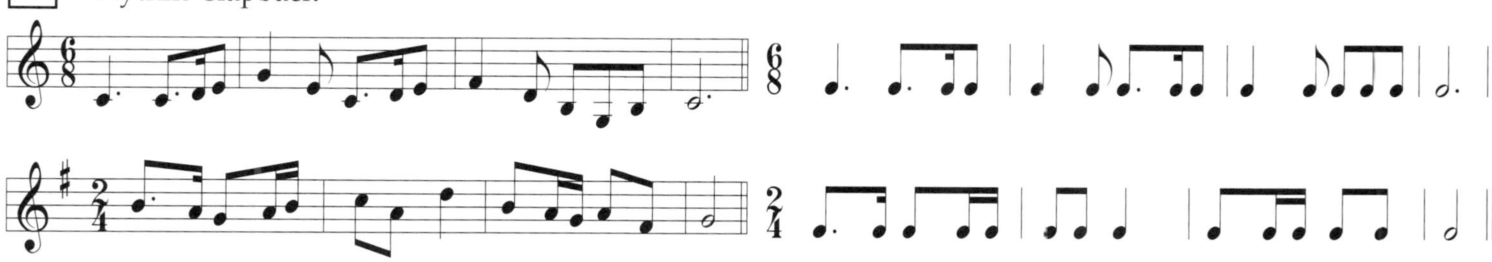

B Interval Identification

perfect 4A | major 2A | major 3B | perfect 5B | minor 3B | major 3A | minor 6A | perfect 8A

C Chord Identification

minor | major | minor | minor | minor | minor

D Melody Playback

Session 29

A Rhythm Clapback

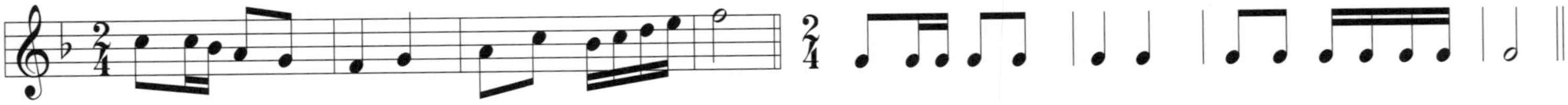

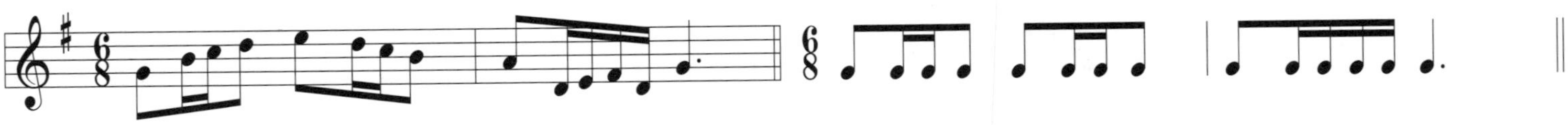

B Interval Identification

minor 3A | major 6A | perfect 8A | perfect 4B | major 3B | major 2A | minor 3B | minor 6B

C Chord Identification

major | minor | major | major | minor | major

D Melody Playback

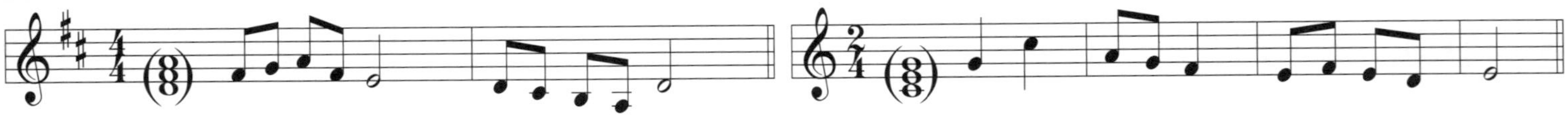

Session 30

A Rhythm Clapback

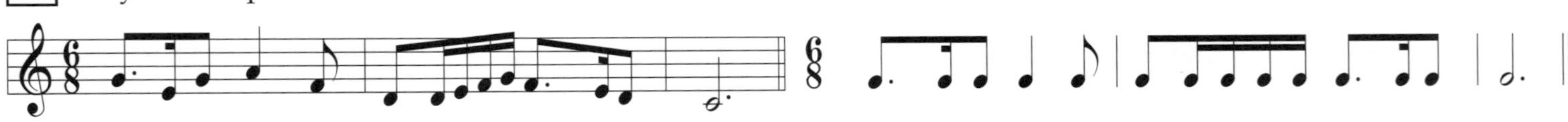

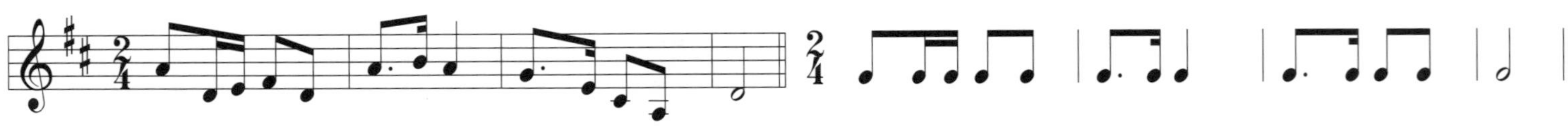

B Interval Identification

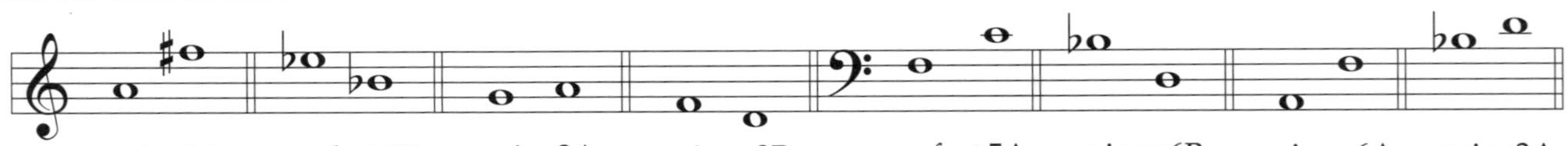

major 6A | perfect 4B | major 2A | minor 3B | perfect 5A | minor 6B | minor 6A | major 3A

C Chord Identification

major | minor | minor | minor | major | minor

D Melody Playback

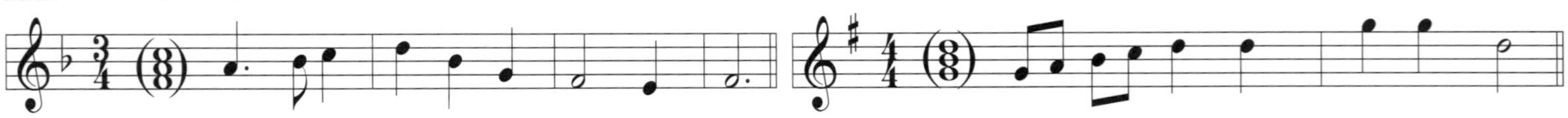

Session 31

A Rhythm Clapback

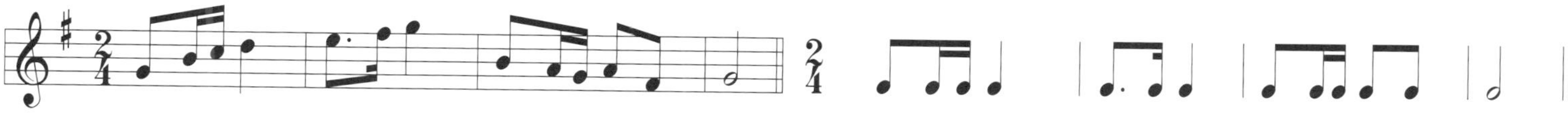

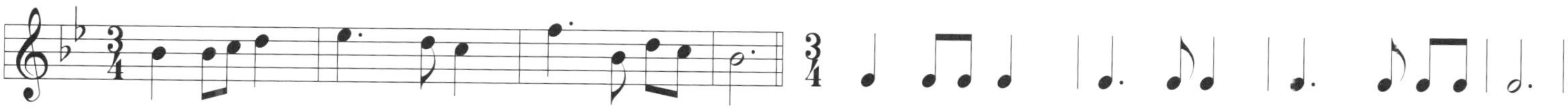

B Interval Identification

minor 6A perfect 8B major 3A minor 6B major 2A major 3B perfect 4A major 6A

C Chord Identification

major major minor minor major major

D Melody Playback

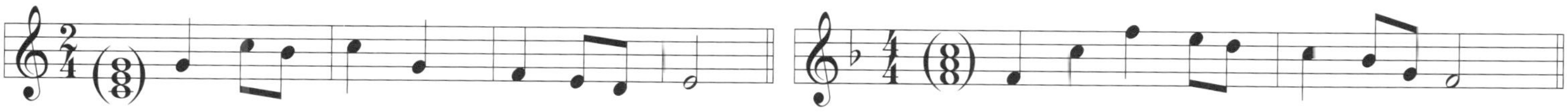

Session 32

A Rhythm Clapback

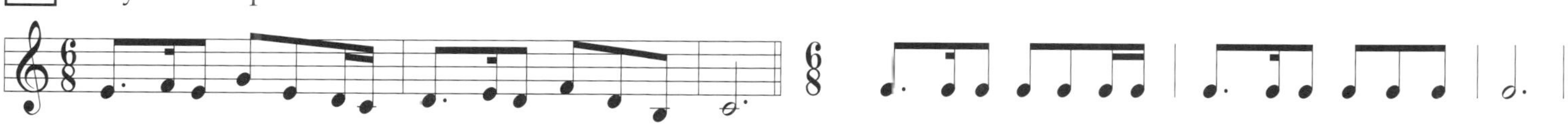

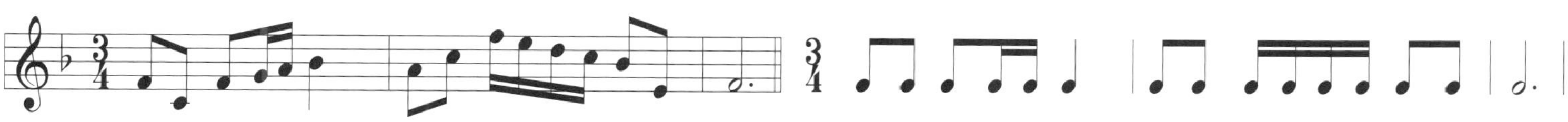

B Interval Identification

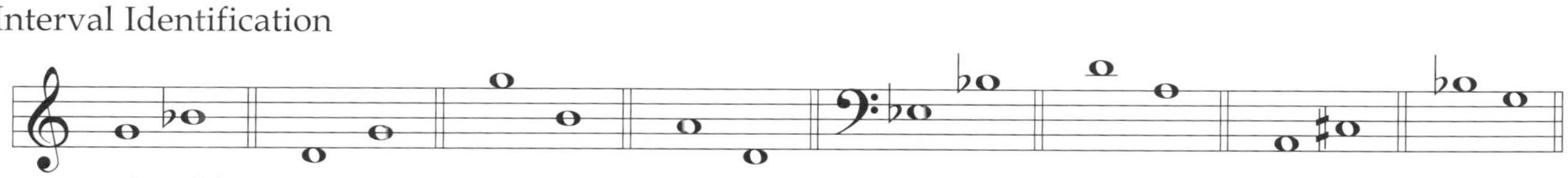

minor 3A perfect 4A minor 6B perfect 5B perfect 5A perfect 4B major 3A minor 3B

C Chord Identification

minor major minor major major minor

D Melody Playback

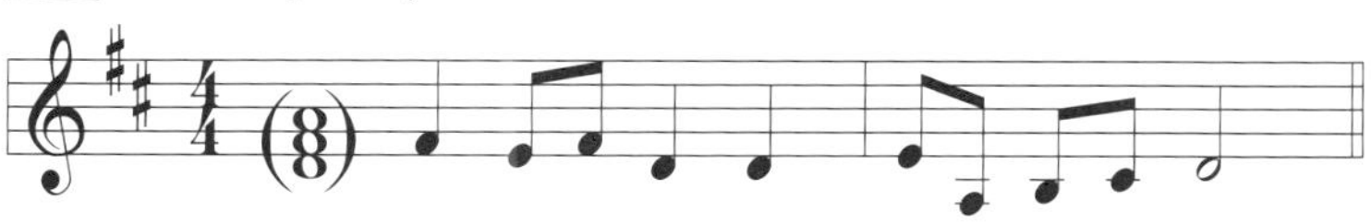

Session 33

A Rhythm Clapback

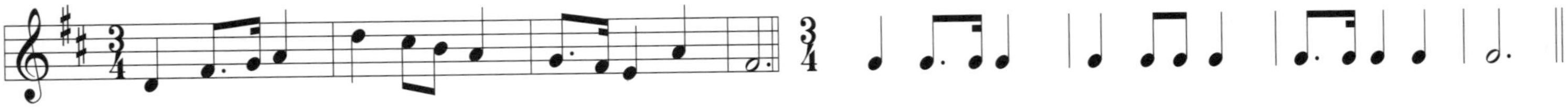

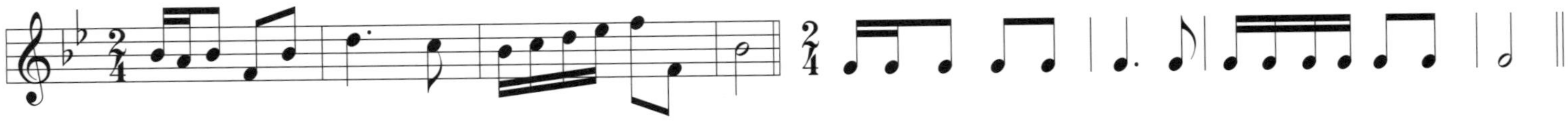

B Interval Identification

C Chord Identification

D Melody Playback

Session 34

A Rhythm Clapback

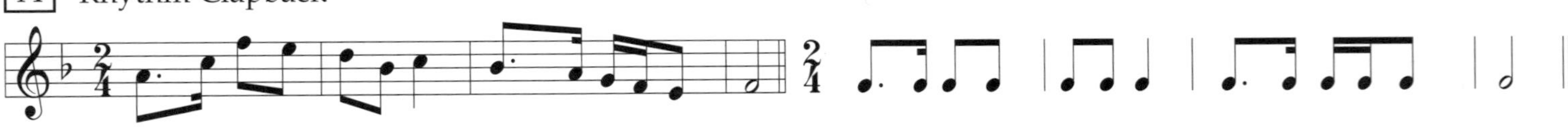

B Interval Identification

C Chord Identification

D Melody Playback

Session 35

A Rhythm Clapback

B Interval Identification

C Chord Identification

D Melody Playback

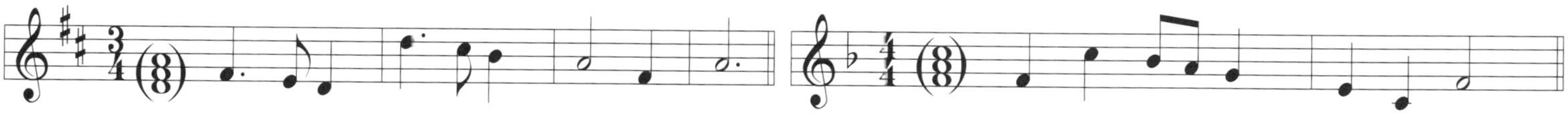

Session 36

A Rhythm Clapback

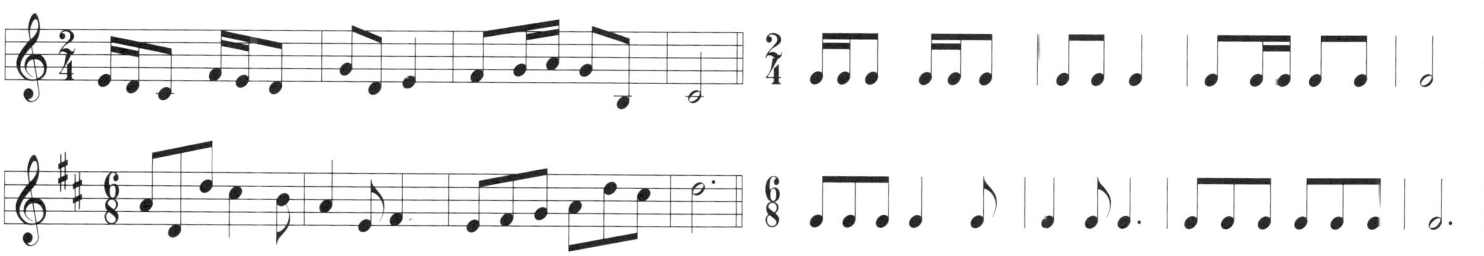

B Interval Identification

C Chord Identification

D Melody Playback

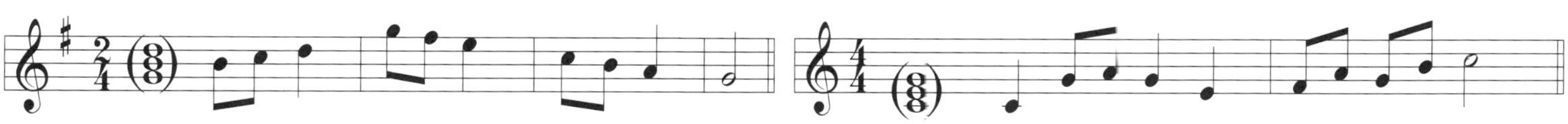

Session 37

A Rhythm Clapback

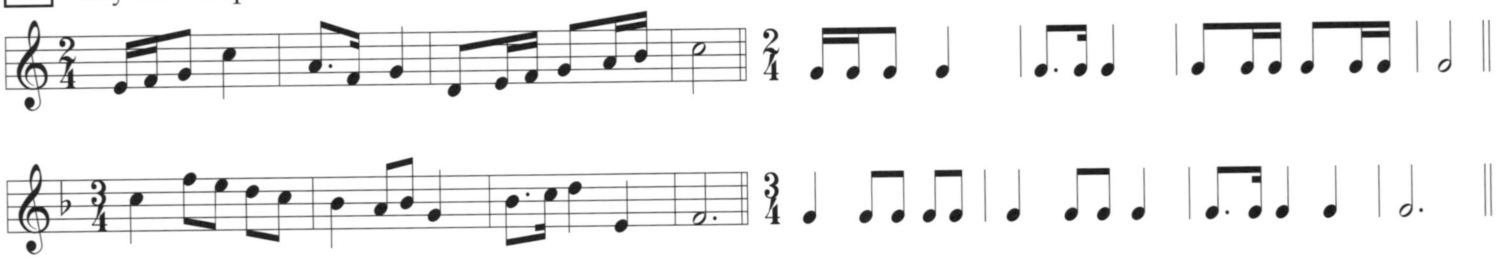

B Interval Identification

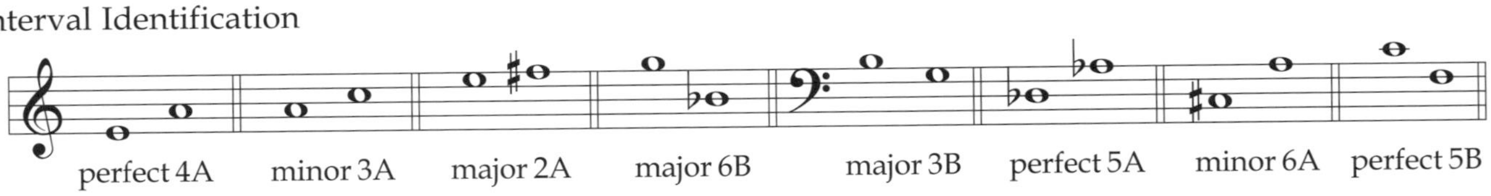

C Chord Identification

D Melody Playback

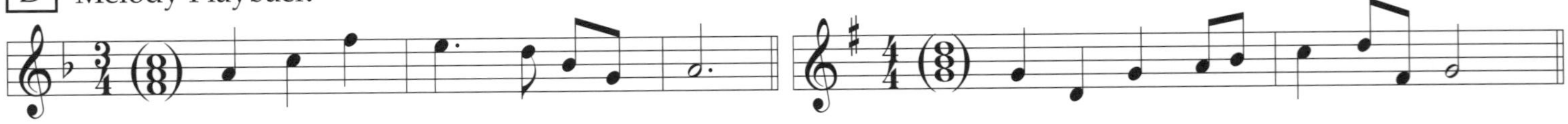

Session 38

A Rhythm Clapback

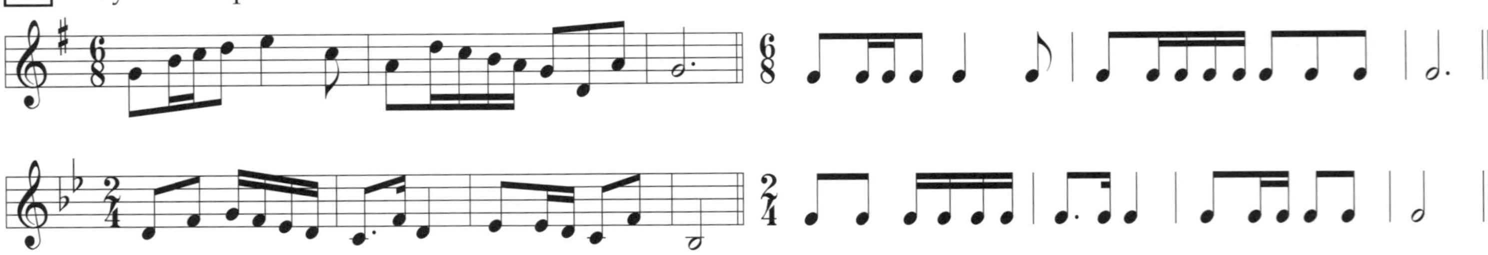

B Interval Identification

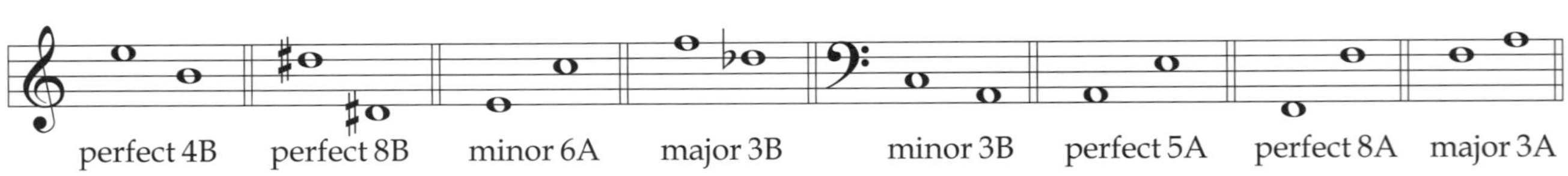

C Chord Identification

D Melody Playback

Session 39

A Rhythm Clapback

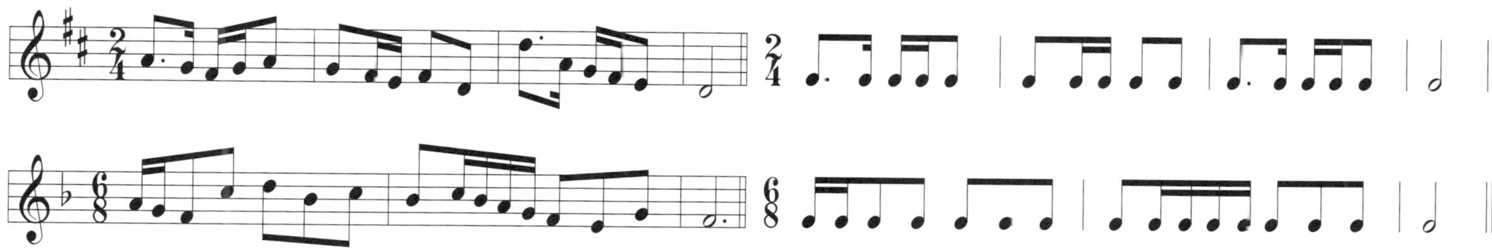

B Interval Identification

minor 6B | major 3A | perfect 4A | minor 3A | major 6A | minor 3B | perfect 8B | major 6A

C Chord Identification

major | major | major | major | minor | major

D Melody Playback

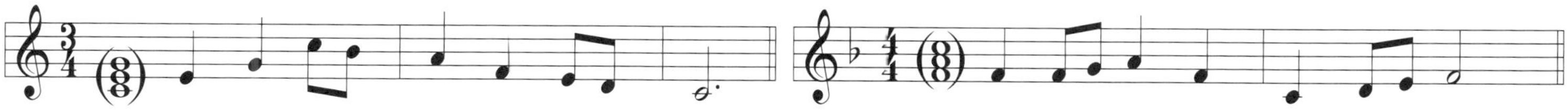

Session 40

A Rhythm Clapback

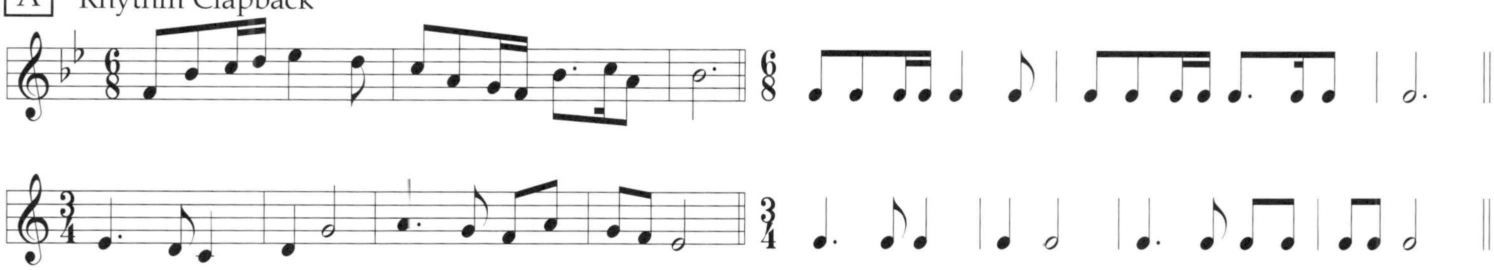

B Interval Identification

perfect 5A | major 2A | major 3B | perfect 4A | minor 6A | minor 3B | perfect 8A | major 3A

C Chord Identification

minor | major | minor | minor | minor | minor

D Melody Playback

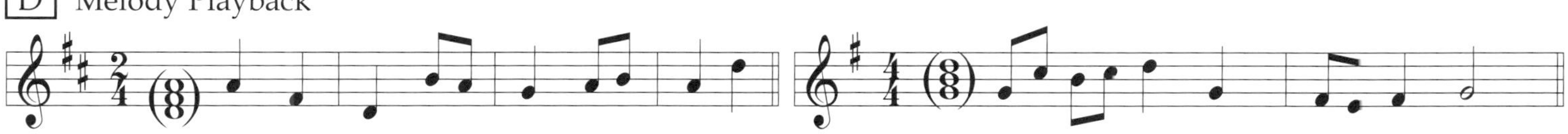

Session 41

A Rhythm Clapback

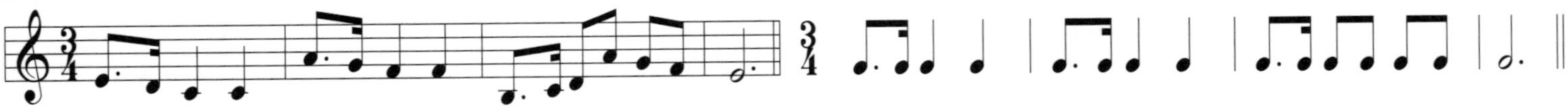

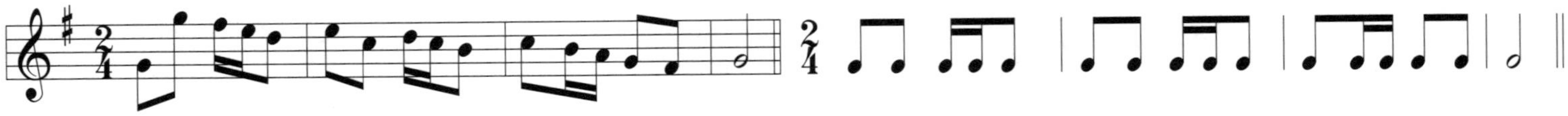

B Interval Identification

C Chord Identification

D Melody Playback

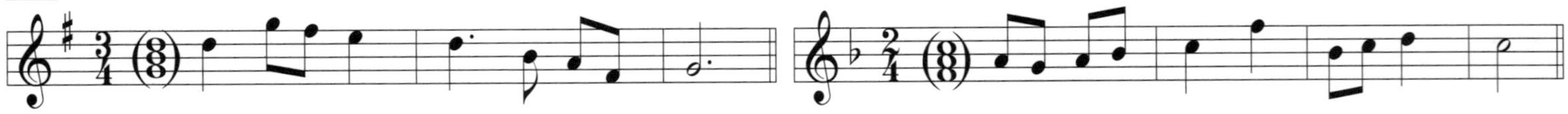

Session 42

A Rhythm Clapback

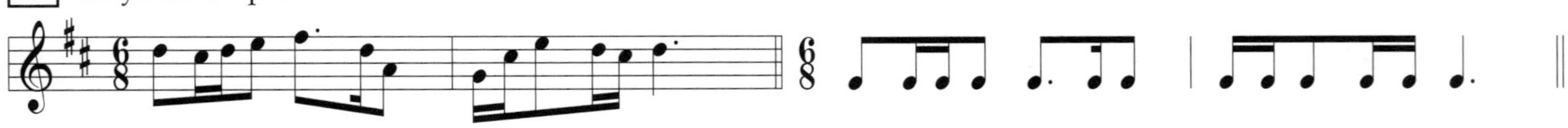

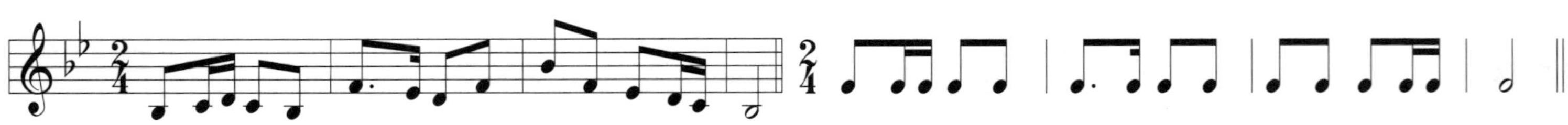

B Interval Identification

C Chord Identification

D Melody Playback

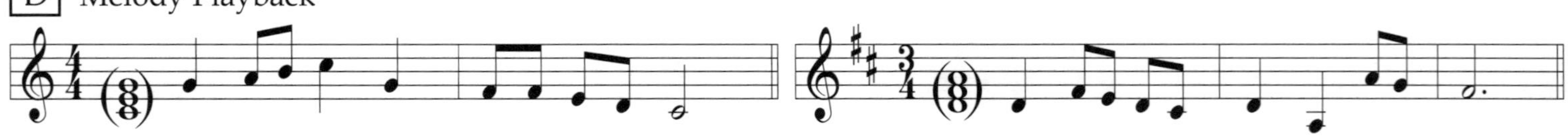

Session 43

A Rhythm Clapback

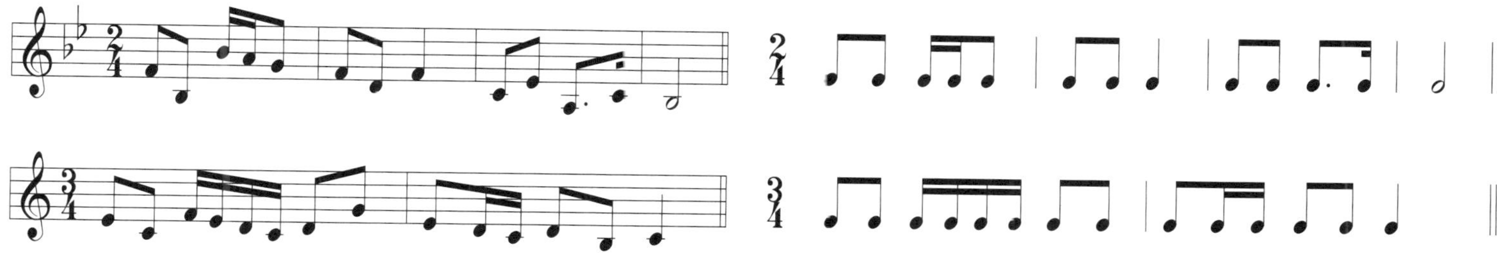

B Interval Identification

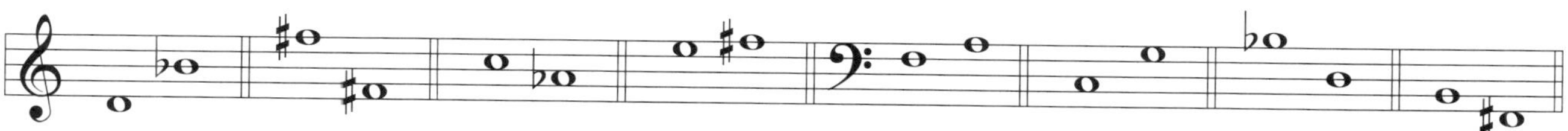

minor 6A | perfect 8B | major 3B | major 2A | major 3A | perfect 5A | minor 6B | perfect 4B

C Chord Identification

minor | major | minor | minor | minor | major

D Melody Playback

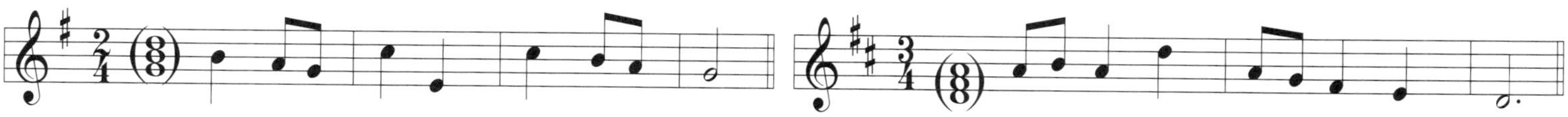

Session 44

A Rhythm Clapback

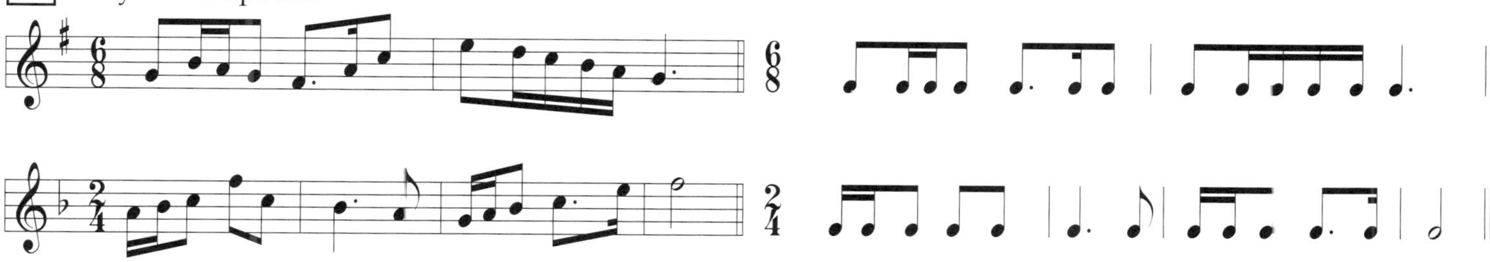

B Interval Identification

major 2A | major 6A | minor 3B | perfect 5B | perfect 4B | minor 3A | perfect 5A | minor 6B

C Chord Identification

major | minor | major | major | minor | major

D Melody Playback

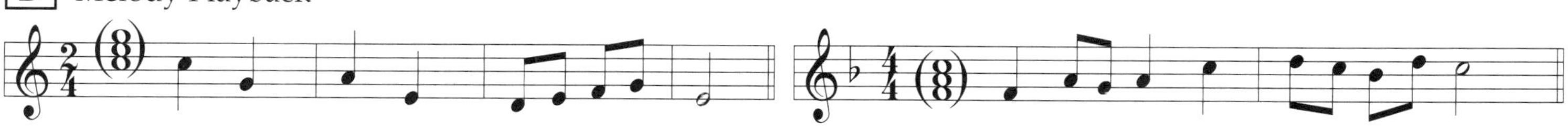

Session 45

A Rhythm Clapback

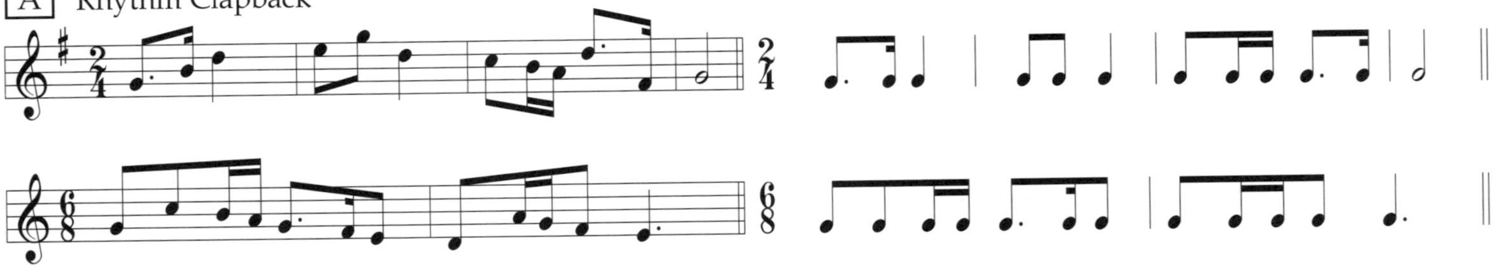

B Interval Identification

C Chord Identification

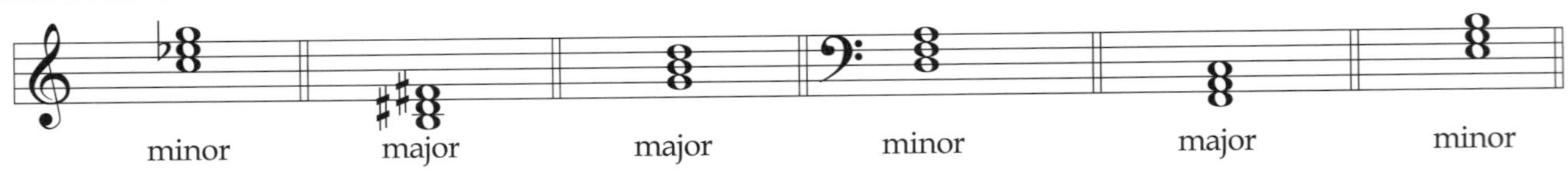

D Melody Playback

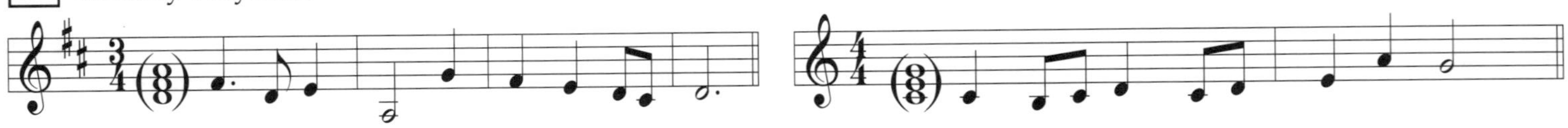

Session 46

A Rhythm Clapback

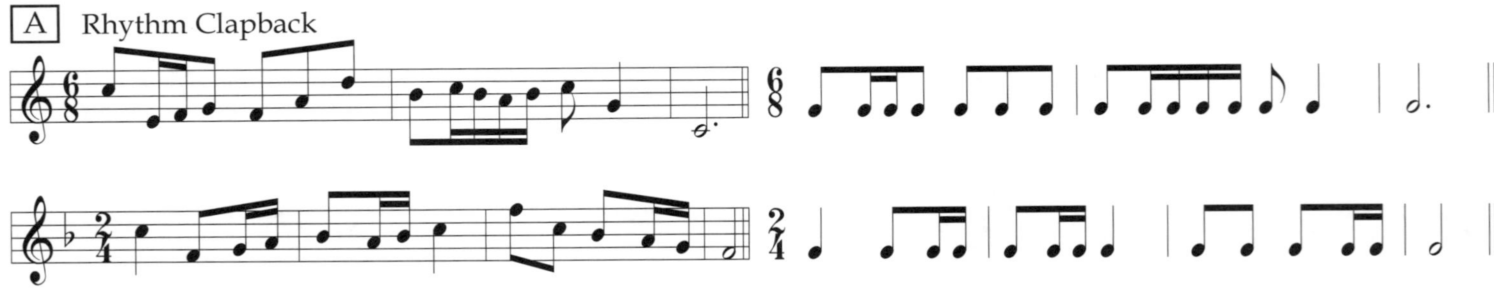

B Interval Identification

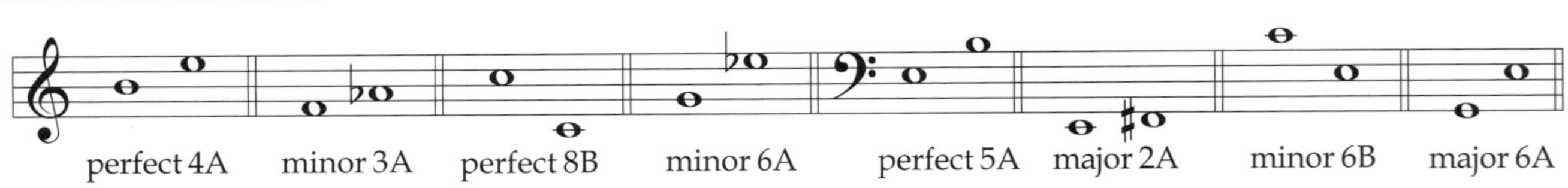

C Chord Identification

D Melody Playback

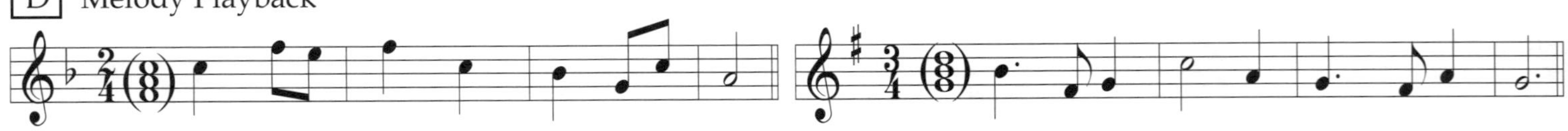

Session 47

A Rhythm Clapback

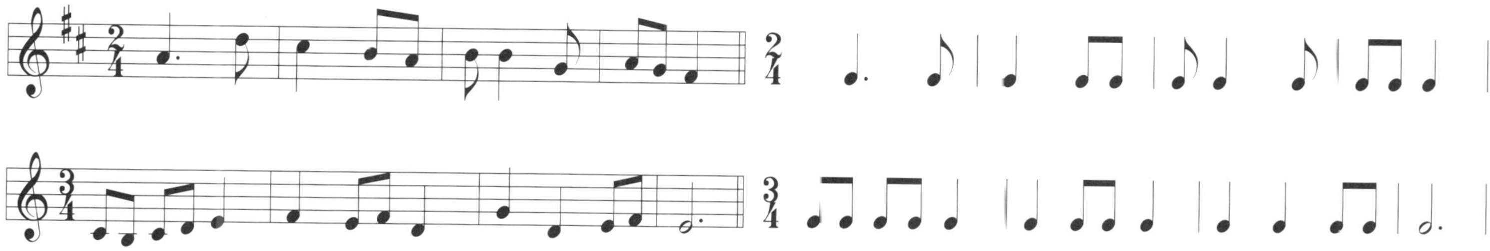

B Interval Identification

minor 6B | perfect 8A | major 3B | major 6A | major 2A | minor 6A | perfect 4B | minor 3B

C Chord Identification

minor | minor | major | major | minor | major

D Melody Playback

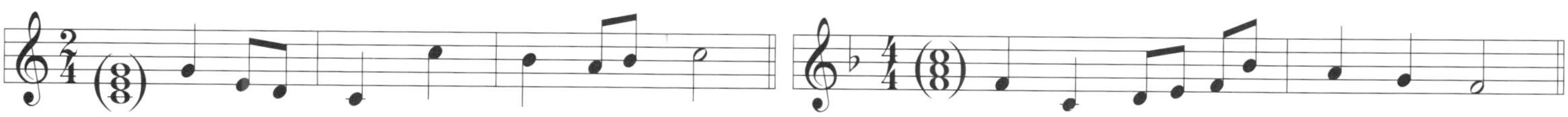

Session 48

A Rhythm Clapback

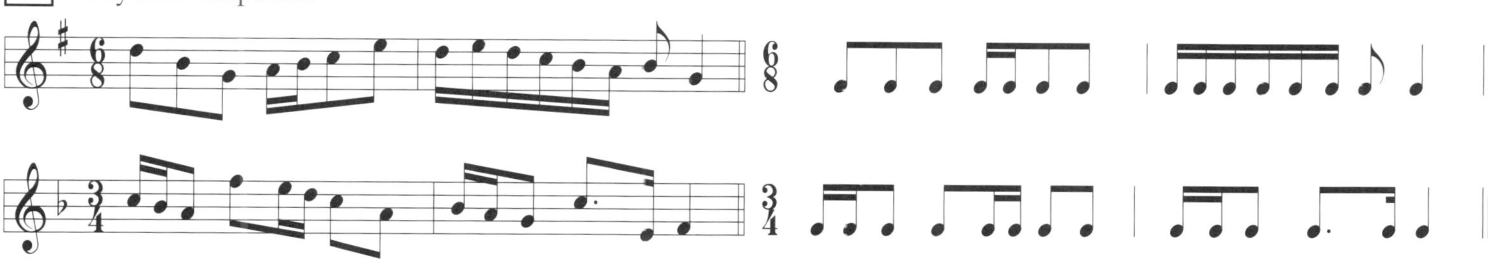

B Interval Identification

perfect 4A | perfect 8B | perfect 5A | minor 3A | perfect 5B | major 3A | minor 6A | major 3B

C Chord Identification

major | minor | major | minor | major | minor

D Melody Playback

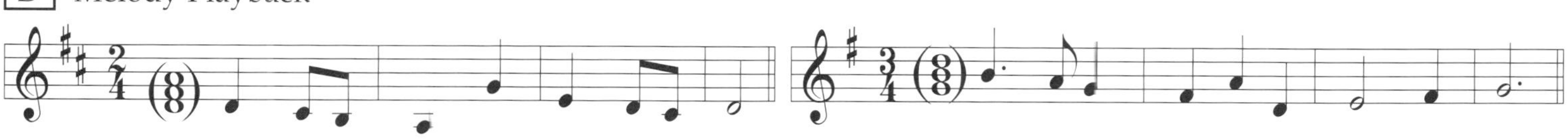

Additional Exercises

Rhythm Clapback Exercises

NOTE: These exercises are NOT recorded on the CDs. Refer to page 7 "Using the Book Only Exercises"

Additional Exercises

Interval Identification Exercises

NOTE: These exercises are NOT recorded on the CDs. Refer to page 7 “Using the Book Only Exercises”

Additional Exercises

Chord Identification Exercises

NOTE: These exercises are NOT recorded on the CDs. Refer to page 7 “Using the Book Only Exercises”

Additional Exercises

Melody Playback Exercises

NOTE: These exercises are NOT recorded on the CDs. Refer to page 7 "Using the Book Only Exercises"

Worksheets Sessions 1 - 8

Session 1

Page 10
Disk 1 Track 2

Score /40

Rhythm Clapback	1	2
	$\frac{3}{4}$	$\frac{2}{4}$

Interval Identification	1	2	3	4	5	6	7	8
	p4	min 3	maj 6	p5	p8	maj 2	min 6	maj 3

Chord Identification	1	2	3	4	5	6
	minor	maj	ma	min	maj	min

Melody Playback	1	2
	F major	C major

Session 2

Page 10
Disk 1 Track 3

Score /40

Rhythm Clapback	1	2
	$\frac{2}{4}$	$\frac{6}{8}$

Interval Identification	1	2	3	4	5	6	7	8
	min 6	maj 2	p5	min 3	p8	maj 3	maj 6	p4

Chord Identification	1	2	3	4	5	6
	maj	min	maj	maj	min	min

Melody Playback	1	2
	G major	C major

Session 3

Page 11
Disk 1 Track 4

Score /40

Rhythm Clapback	1	2
	$\frac{6}{8}$	$\frac{3}{4}$

Interval Identification	1	2	3	4	5	6	7	8
	maj 3	p5	min 6	maj 2	p4	min 3	p8	maj 6

Chord Identification	1	2	3	4	5	6
	min	maj	min	min	maj	maj

Melody Playback	1	2
	D major	F major

Session 4

Page 11
Disk 1 Track 5

Score /40

Rhythm Clapback	1	2
	$\frac{2}{4}$	$\frac{6}{8}$

Interval Identification	1	2	3	4	5	6	7	8
	maj 6	min 3	p4	maj 2	maj 3	p8	min 6	p5

Chord Identification	1	2	3	4	5	6
	min	maj	min	maj	maj	min

Melody Playback	1	2
	G major	C major

Session 5

Page 12
Disk 1 Track 6

Score /40

Rhythm Clapback	1	2
	$\frac{2}{4}$	$\frac{3}{4}$

Interval Identification	1	2	3	4	5	6	7	8
	min 6	maj 3	maj 2	p5	min 3	p4	maj 6	p8

Chord Identification	1	2	3	4	5	6
	min	maj	min	maj	min	maj

Melody Playback	1	2
	F major	G major

Session 6

Page 12
Disk 1 Track 7

Score /40

Rhythm Clapback	1	2
	$\frac{6}{8}$	$\frac{2}{4}$

Interval Identification	1	2	3	4	5	6	7	8
	maj 3	p	min 6	min 3	p	p	maj 6	maj 2

Chord Identification	1	2	3	4	5	6
	maj	min	min	maj	maj	min

Melody Playback	1	2
	C major	D major

Session 7

Page 13
Disk 1 Track 8

Score /40

Rhythm Clapback	1	2
	$\frac{2}{4}$	$\frac{6}{8}$

Interval Identification	1	2	3	4	5	6	7	8
	p8	maj 2	min 6	p4	min 3	p5	maj 6	maj 3

Chord Identification	1	2	3	4	5	6
	maj	maj	min	min	major	min

Melody Playback	1	2
	C major	F major

Session 8

Page 13
Disk 1 Track 9

Score /40

Rhythm Clapback	1	2
	$\frac{6}{8}$	$\frac{3}{4}$

Interval Identification	1	2	3	4	5	6	7	8
	min 2	maj 2	p4	p8	min 6	maj 3	min 6	p5

Chord Identification	1	2	3	4	5	6
	maj	min	maj	maj	min	min

Melody Playback	1	2
	D major	G major

Worksheets Sessions 9 - 16

Session 9
Page 14
Disk 1 Track 10

Score /40

Rhythm Clapback	1	2
	3/4	2/4

Interval Identification	1	2	3	4	5	6	7	8
	maj 3	P5	min 3	min 6	P4	maj 6	P8	maj 7

Chord Identification	1	2	3	4	5	6
	min	maj	min	maj	maj	min

Melody Playback	1	2
	G major	F major

Session 10
Page 14
Disk 1 Track 11

Score /40

Rhythm Clapback	1	2
	6/8	2/4

Interval Identification	1	2	3	4	5	6	7	8
	P8	min 3	P5	maj 6	maj 7	P4	min 6	maj 3

Chord Identification	1	2	3	4	5	6
	maj	min	min	maj	min	maj

Melody Playback	1	2
	C major	D major

Session 11
Page 15
Disk 1 Track 12

Score /40

Rhythm Clapback	1	2
	2/4	3/4

Interval Identification	1	2	3	4	5	6	7	8
	min 3	P8	maj 3	min 6	maj 7	P4	maj 6	P5

Chord Identification	1	2	3	4	5	6
	min	maj	maj	min	maj	min

Melody Playback	1	2
	G major	D major

Session 12
Page 15
Disk 1 Track 13

Score /40

Rhythm Clapback	1	2
	6/8	2/4

Interval Identification	1	2	3	4	5	6	7	8
	P4	maj 3	maj 7	P5	min 6	P8	maj 6	min 3

Chord Identification	1	2	3	4	5	6
	min	min	maj	maj	min	maj

Melody Playback	1	2
	C major	F major

Session 13
Page 16
Disk 1 Track 14

Score /40

Rhythm Clapback	1	2
	2/4	6/8

Interval Identification	1	2	3	4	5	6	7	8
	min 3	maj 6	P4	min 3	P8	P5	maj 6	maj 7

Chord Identification	1	2	3	4	5	6
	maj	min	maj	maj	min	maj

Melody Playback	1	2
	D major	C major

Session 14
Page 16
Disk 1 Track 15

Score /40

Rhythm Clapback	1	2
	6/8	2/4

Interval Identification	1	2	3	4	5	6	7	8
	P5	maj 6	min 3	min 6	P8	maj 7	maj 3	P4

Chord Identification	1	2	3	4	5	6
	min	maj	maj	min	min	min

Melody Playback	1	2
	F major	G major

Session 15
Page 17
Disk 1 Track 16

Score /40

Rhythm Clapback	1	2
	2/4	3/4

Interval Identification	1	2	3	4	5	6	7	8
	P8	min 6	P4	maj 3	maj 7	maj 6	P5	min 3

Chord Identification	1	2	3	4	5	6
	min	maj	maj	maj	min	maj

Melody Playback	1	2
	C major	F major

Session 16
Page 17
Disk 1 Track 17

Score /40

Rhythm Clapback	1	2
	6/8	3/4

Interval Identification	1	2	3	4	5	6	7	8
	maj 6	P	min 3	P	maj 7	P	min 6	maj 3

Chord Identification	1	2	3	4	5	6
	maj	min	maj	min	min	maj

Melody Playback	1	2
	D major	G major

Worksheets Sessions 17 - 24

Session 17

Page 18 · Disk 1 Track 18

Rhythm Clapback	1	2
	$\frac{3}{4}$	$\frac{2}{4}$

Interval Identification	1	2	3	4	5	6	7	8
	maj 3	P5	min 6	maj 2	P8	min 3	P4	maj 6

Chord Identification	1	2	3	4	5	6
	maj	min	min	maj	maj	min

Melody Playback	1	2
	F major	C major

Score /40

Session 18

Page 18 · Disk 1 Track 19

Rhythm Clapback	1	2
	$\frac{2}{4}$	$\frac{6}{8}$

Interval Identification	1	2	3	4	5	6	7	8
	P8	maj 3	P5	min 6	maj 2	P4	maj 6	min 3

Chord Identification	1	2	3	4	5	6
	maj	min	maj	min	maj	maj

Melody Playback	1	2
	G major	C major

Score /40

Session 19

Page 19 · Disk 1 Track 20

Rhythm Clapback	1	2
	$\frac{6}{8}$	$\frac{3}{4}$

Interval Identification	1	2	3	4	5	6	7	8
	maj 6	P8	min 3	P5	maj 2	min 6	maj 3	P4

Chord Identification	1	2	3	4	5	6
	maj	maj	min	min	min	maj

Melody Playback	1	2
	D major	F major

Score /40

Session 20

Page 19 · Disk 1 Track 21

Rhythm Clapback	1	2
	$\frac{2}{4}$	$\frac{6}{8}$

Interval Identification	1	2	3	4	5	6	7	8
	maj 3	min 6	P5	min 3	P8	maj 2	P4	maj 6

Chord Identification	1	2	3	4	5	6
	min	maj	maj	min	min	maj

Melody Playback	1	2
	G major	C major

Score /40

Session 21

Page 20 · Disk 1 Track 22

Rhythm Clapback	1	2
	$\frac{2}{4}$	$\frac{3}{4}$

Interval Identification	1	2	3	4	5	6	7	8
	P8	maj 3	min 6	maj 2	P4	P5	min 3	maj 6

Chord Identification	1	2	3	4	5	6
	min	maj	min	min	maj	maj

Melody Playback	1	2
	F major	G major

Score /40

Session 22

Page 20 · Disk 1 Track 23

Rhythm Clapback	1	2
	$\frac{6}{8}$	$\frac{2}{4}$

Interval Identification	1	2	3	4	5	6	7	8
	maj 3	P4	min 3	P8	maj 2	P5	maj 6	min 6

Chord Identification	1	2	3	4	5	6
	min	maj	maj	min	maj	min

Melody Playback	1	2
	C major	D major

Score /40

Session 23

Page 21 · Disk 1 Track 24

Rhythm Clapback	1	2
	$\frac{2}{4}$	$\frac{6}{8}$

Interval Identification	1	2	3	4	5	6	7	8
	P4	min 6	maj 2	P8	min 3	maj 6	P5	maj 6

Chord Identification	1	2	3	4	5	6
	maj	min	min	maj	min	maj

Melody Playback	1	2
	C major	F major

Score /40

Session 24

Page 21 · Disk 1 Track 25

Rhythm Clapback	1	2
	$\frac{6}{8}$	$\frac{3}{4}$

Interval Identification	1	2	3	4	5	6	7	8
	maj 6	P5	maj 2	min 3	P8	min 6	maj 3	P4

Chord Identification	1	2	3	4	5	6
	maj	min	maj	min	min	maj

Melody Playback	1	2
	D major	G major

Score /40

Worksheets Sessions 25 - 32

Session 25

Page 22
Disk 2 Track 1

Score /40

Rhythm Clapback	1	2
	3/4	2/4

Interval Identification	1	2	3	4	5	6	7	8
	min 6	maj 3	P4	min 3	P8	maj 7	P5	maj 6

Chord Identification	1	2	3	4	5	6
	maj	min	maj	maj	min	min

Melody Playback	1	2
	G major	**F** major

Session 26

Page 22
Disk 2 Track 2

Score /40

Rhythm Clapback	1	2
	6/8	2/4

Interval Identification	1	2	3	4	5	6	7	8
	maj 6	P4	P5	min 3	maj 7	P8	min 6	maj 3

Chord Identification	1	2	3	4	5	6
	min	maj	maj	min	maj	min

Melody Playback	1	2
	C major	**D** major

Session 27

Page 23
Disk 2 Track 3

Score /40

Rhythm Clapback	1	2
	2/4	3/4

Interval Identification	1	2	3	4	5	6	7	8
	maj 6	P4	maj 3	P8	min 3	maj 7	P5	min 6

Chord Identification	1	2	3	4	5	6
	maj	min	min	maj	maj	min

Melody Playback	1	2
	G major	**D** major

Session 28

Page 23
Disk 2 Track 4

Score /40

Rhythm Clapback	1	2
	6/8	2/4

Interval Identification	1	2	3	4	5	6	7	8
	P8	min 6	maj 7	P5	min 3	maj 6	maj 3	P4

Chord Identification	1	2	3	4	5	6
	min	maj	maj	maj	min	min

Melody Playback	1	2
	C major	**F** major

Session 29

Page 24
Disk 2Track 5

Score /40

Rhythm Clapback	1	2
	2/4	6/8

Interval Identification	1	2	3	4	5	6	7	8
	min 6	maj 7	P5	min 3	P8	maj 6	P4	maj 3

Chord Identification	1	2	3	4	5	6
	maj	min	min	maj	maj	maj

Melody Playback	1	2
	D major	**C** major

Session 30

Page 24
Disk 2 Track 6

Score /40

Rhythm Clapback	1	2
	6/8	2/4

Interval Identification	1	2	3	4	5	6	7	8
	P8	maj 6	P5	min 3	maj 7	P4	min 6	maj 3

Chord Identification	1	2	3	4	5	6
	min	min	maj	maj	min	maj

Melody Playback	1	2
	F major	**G** major

Session 31

Page 25
Disk 2 Track 7

Score /40

Rhythm Clapback	1	2
	2/4	3/4

Interval Identification	1	2	3	4	5	6	7	8
	maj 7	P4	min 3	P8	maj 6	P5	min 6	maj 3

Chord Identification	1	2	3	4	5	6
	maj	min	maj	min	min	maj

Melody Playback	1	2
	C major	**F** major

Session 32

Page 25
Disk 2 Track 8

Score /40

Rhythm Clapback	1	2
	6/8	3/4

Interval Identification	1	2	3	4	5	6	7	8
	min 6	maj 3	P5	maj 7	min 3	P8	maj 6	P4

Chord Identification	1	2	3	4	5	6
	maj	maj	min	maj	min	min

Melody Playback	1	2
	D major	**G** major

Worksheets Sessions 33 - 40

Session 33
Page 26
Disk 2 Track 9

Rhythm Clapback	1	2
	3/4	2/4

Interval Identification	1	2	3	4	5	6	7	8
	min 3	maj 7	P5	min 3	maj 3	P8	maj 6	P4

Score /40

Chord Identification	1	2	3	4	5	6
	maj	min	maj	min	min	maj

Melody Playback	1	2
	F major	C major

Session 34
Page 26
Disk 2 Track 10

Rhythm Clapback	1	2
	2/4	6/8

Interval Identification	1	2	3	4	5	6	7	8
	maj 6	P8	min 3	P4	maj 7	min 6	P5	maj 3

Score /40

Chord Identification	1	2	3	4	5	6
	min	maj	min	min	maj	maj

Melody Playback	1	2
	G major	C major

Session 35
Page 27
Disk 2 Track 11

Rhythm Clapback	1	2
	6/8	3/4

Interval Identification	1	2	3	4	5	6	7	8
	P5	min 3	maj 6	P8	min 6	P4	maj 7	maj 3

Score /40

Chord Identification	1	2	3	4	5	6
	maj	maj	min	maj	min	maj

Melody Playback	1	2
	D major	F major

Session 36
Page 27
Disk 2 Track 12

Rhythm Clapback	1	2
	2/4	6/8

Interval Identification	1	2	3	4	5	6	7	8
	min 6	P5	maj 3	maj 7	P8	min 3	maj 6	P4

Score /40

Chord Identification	1	2	3	4	5	6
	min	maj	min	min	maj	maj

Melody Playback	1	2
	G major	C major

Session 37
Page 28
Disk 2 Track 13

Rhythm Clapback	1	2
	2/4	3/4

Interval Identification	1	2	3	4	5	6	7	8
	min 6	maj 3	P5	P8	maj 7	P4	maj 6	min 3

Score /40

Chord Identification	1	2	3	4	5	6
	maj	min	maj	min	min	maj

Melody Playback	1	2
	F major	G major

Session 38
Page 28
Disk 2 Track 14

Rhythm Clapback	1	2
	6/8	2/4

Interval Identification	1	2	3	4	5	6	7	8
	min 6	P8	min 3	maj 6	P4	maj 7	P5	maj 3

Score /40

Chord Identification	1	2	3	4	5	6
	min	min	maj	maj	min	maj

Melody Playback	1	2
	C major	D major

Session 39
Page 29
Disk 2 Track 15

Rhythm Clapback	1	2
	2/4	6/8

Interval Identification	1	2	3	4	5	6	7	8
	maj 7	min 3	P5	min 6	P4	maj 3	maj 6	P8

Score /40

Chord Identification	1	2	3	4	5	6
	maj	min	maj	min	min	maj

Melody Playback	1	2
	C major	F major

Session 40
Page 29
Disk 2 Track 16

Rhythm Clapback	1	2
	6/8	3/4

Interval Identification	1	2	3	4	5	6	7	8
	P5	min 6	P8	min 3	maj 3	P4	maj 7	maj 6

Score /40

Chord Identification	1	2	3	4	5	6
	maj	min	min	maj	maj	min

Melody Playback	1	2
	D major	G major

Worksheets Sessions 41 - 48

Session 41

Page 30
Disk 2 Track 17

Score: /40

Rhythm Clapback	1	2
	3/4	2/4

Interval Identification	1	2	3	4	5	6	7	8
	min 6	P8	min 3	P5	maj 6	maj 2	P4	maj 3

Chord Identification	1	2	3	4	5	6
	maj	maj	min	min	maj	maj

Melody Playback	1	2
	G major	F major

Session 42

Page 30
Disk 2 Track 18

Score: /40

Rhythm Clapback	1	2
	6/8	2/4

Interval Identification	1	2	3	4	5	6	7	8
	maj 6	P5	min 6	maj 7	P8	min 3	maj 3	P4

Chord Identification	1	2	3	4	5	6
	min	maj	min	min	maj	min

Melody Playback	1	2
	C major	D major

Session 43

Page 31
Disk 2 Track 19

Score: /40

Rhythm Clapback	1	2
	2/4	3/4

Interval Identification	1	2	3	4	5	6	7	8
	maj 3	P8	min 6	P5	min 3	maj 2	P4	maj 6

Chord Identification	1	2	3	4	5	6
	maj	maj	min	maj	min	maj

Melody Playback	1	2
	G major	D major

Session 44

Page 31
Disk 2 Track 20

Score: /40

Rhythm Clapback	1	2
	6/8	2/4

Interval Identification	1	2	3	4	5	6	7	8
	maj 3	maj 6	P5	min 3	P8	P4	min 6	maj 2

Chord Identification	1	2	3	4	5	6
	min	min	maj	maj	min	maj

Melody Playback	1	2
	C major	F major

Session 45

Page 32
Disk 2 Track 21

Score: /40

Rhythm Clapback	1	2
	2/4	6/8

Interval Identification	1	2	3	4	5	6	7	8
	maj 6	maj 3	P4	min 6	P8	maj 2	min 3	P5

Chord Identification	1	2	3	4	5	6
	min	min	min	maj	maj	maj

Melody Playback	1	2
	D major	C major

Session 46

Page 32
Disk 2 Track 22

Score: /40

Rhythm Clapback	1	2
	6/8	2/4

Interval Identification	1	2	3	4	5	6	7	8
	min 3	P8	maj 3	maj 2	min 6	P4	maj 6	P5

Chord Identification	1	2	3	4	5	6
	min	maj	maj	min	min	maj

Melody Playback	1	2
	F major	G major

Session 47

Page 33
Disk 2 Track 23

Score: /40

Rhythm Clapback	1	2
	2/4	3/4

Interval Identification	1	2	3	4	5	6	7	8
	P5	maj 3	min 6	P8	maj 6	maj 2	P4	min 3

Chord Identification	1	2	3	4	5	6
	maj	min	min	maj	maj	min

Melody Playback	1	2
	C major	F major

Session 48

Page 33
Disk 2 Track 24

Score: /40

Rhythm Clapback	1	2
	6/8	3/4

Interval Identification	1	2	3	4	5	6	7	8
	min 3	maj 6	P8	min 6	maj 2	P4	maj 3	P5

Chord Identification	1	2	3	4	5	6
	maj	min	maj	min	min	maj

Melody Playback	1	2
	D major	G major

Summer

Claire Llewellyn

SIMON & SCHUSTER
YOUNG BOOKS

Notes for parents and teachers
This book has a theme that threads its way through the subject of the book. It does not aim to deal with the topic comprehensively; rather it aims to provoke thought and discussion. Each page heading makes a simple statement about the illustration which is then amplified and questioned by the text. Material in this book is particularly relevant to the following sections of the National Curriculum for England and Wales:

English: AT1 levels 1–2, AT2 levels 1–3
Geography: AT5 levels 1–3
Science: AT2 levels 1–3, AT9 levels 1–2, AT16 levels 1–3

In Scotland the proposals of the Scottish Education Department apply.

TAKE ONE has been researched and compiled by Simon & Schuster Young Books. We are very grateful for the support and guidance provided by our advisory panel of professional educationalists in the course of the production.

Advisory panel:
Colin Pidgeon, Headteacher
Wheatfields Junior School, St Albans
Deirdre Walker, Deputy headteacher
Wheatfields Junior School, St Albans
Judith Clarke, Headteacher
Grove Infants School, Harpenden

A catalogue record for this book
is available from the British Library
ISBN 0 7500 1034 7

Commissioning editor: Daphne Butler
Design: M&M Design Partnership
Photographs: ZEFA except for page 15 Ecoscene and page 21 Camilla Jessel.
Line artwork: Raymond Turvey

First published in Great Britain in 1992
by Simon & Schuster Young Books

Simon & Schuster Young Books
Campus 400, Maylands Avenue
Hemel Hempstead, Herts HP2 7EZ

Printed and bound in Great Britain
by BPCC Hazell Books, Paulton and Aylesbury

Contents

Summer is coming

How can you tell that summer is coming? What changes does the new season bring?

Long days, short nights

Day breaks early in summer. The sun is high in the sky before you're even awake, and it sets long after you're asleep. Evenings are light and warm.

On the other side of the world it's winter. Do you know why?

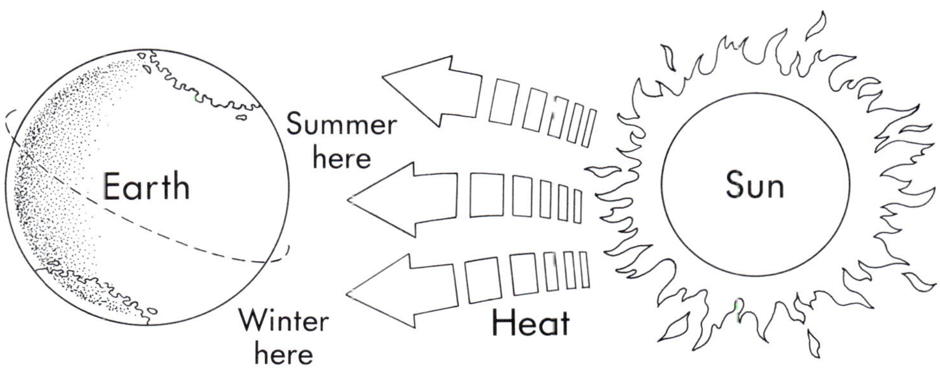

Which half of the Earth is tilted towards the sun?

The weather is warm

In summer, we expect the days to be bright and warm. Sometimes they are a little too warm.

How do you feel on a hot day at school? What do you like to wear? What sort of food do you like to eat?

12

Birds breed here in summer

In early summer, many birds arrive from warmer countries. They come to build a nest and raise their young.

Do you know which birds make these long journeys? Why don't they live in one place?

The trees are growing

Blossom fades on trees as spring turns into summer. Now the new leaves unfold and grow, stretching towards the sun. They are collecting the energy that trees need in order to grow.

Flowers bloom in the sun

Seeds that were sown in the spring have grown into plants. They flower now, making windowboxes bright with colour.

In meadows, tall grasses and wild flowers are wafted by the warm breeze. How were their seeds planted?

Insects collect pollen

Have you ever seen a bush covered with bees? They are feeding. Inside each flower there is a drop of sweet nectar. Bees and other insects feed on this.

As they collect the nectar from flowers, insects brush against a yellow dust, called pollen. It sticks to their body as they fly from flower to flower.

What is pollen, and why is it important?

Summer fruits are ripe

Summer fruits may not last long, but they taste wonderful! Which is your favourite?

Have you ever picked summer fruits yourself? What did you do with them afterwards?

Lazy days

It's so good to be outside in the sun – playing, learning a new sport, having a picnic somewhere, or perhaps just lying on the grass with a book.

How do you like to spend a summer's day?

It's holiday time

Thousands of people go on holiday in the summer. Some go to the seaside. Others like the country. Which do you prefer?

The woman in the picture is putting cream on her son's back. Why? How else can you protect yourself from the sun?

Farmers harvest the crops

Farmers don't go on holiday in the summer. The moment their crops are ripe, they harvest them and bring them safely under cover.

Which crops are harvested by big machines like this?

Autumn is coming

The light is changing. The sun is lower in the sky, and shadows are beginning to lengthen, even at midday.

What other signs tell you that the season is changing? Why does autumn always follow summer?

Index